To Soul Home and Back

RITA BORENSTEIN

TO SOUL HOME AND BACK

RITA BORENSTEIN

ABOUT LIFE BETWEEN LIVES
HYPNOTHERAPY
FOR SPIRITUAL REGRESSION

ISBN 978-91-519-4346-6

www.ritaborenstein.se

Graphic design by Lilla blå tornet, Sweden
www.lillablatornet.se

Cover illustration: Thinkstock

Print version: ISBN 978-91-639-8209-5
E-book: ISBN 978-91-519-4347-3
PrintOnDemand: ISBN 978-91-519-4346-6

You would know the hidden realm
where all souls dwell.
The journey's way lies
through death's misty fell.
Within this timeless passage
a guiding light does dance.
Lost from conscious memory,
but visible in trance.

DR. MICHAEL NEWTON, 1931 – 2016

Content

~

Forewords

~

By **Dr. Dorothea Fuckert M.D.,**
Life Between Lives therapist, mentor of
the Newton Institute and author, Germany

I read Rita Borenstein's book with appreciation and delight and am honored to write this foreword. Rita describes Dr. Michael Newton's "Life Between Lives" (LBL) hypnotherapy as a life-changing spiritual method, in a clear and authentic way. It's a courageous book, as the author relates her personal experiences, including painful ones. She refers colorfully to burnout, dissociation, self-hypnosis, near-death experience and our perception of time and reality.

Rita understands disease and crisis as opportunities. She

describes her path from self-sacrificing "functioning", to finding the calling to her true-life purpose, to healing and to self-love. LBL is a healing method which therapeutically activates a person's super-conscious memories of her all-encompassing being, the Soul: her timeless existence in higher dimensions of light, peace and freedom.

I also appreciate the courage of a surgeon to share his LBL experiences. This academic reveals himself as a human on a spiritual path, and thereby is setting an example for others.

From forty years of medical practice, psychotherapy and countless LBL sessions (including with many colleagues), I estimate that about one third of the physicians in Germany are satisfied with their professional work, another third has found an alternative niche, and at least one third are looking for a way out of a frozen, bureaucratic, loveless system – and are searching for the true purpose of life. They haven't found it in materialistic medicine, nor in society's general alignment with competition, overwork, recognition and prestige. Academics don't usually speak of their spiritual interests and experiences, due to fear of losing credibility. Therefore this story of spiritual advancement through LBL is precious, and more so because they are told by Rita in a loving and refreshing way.

Fortunately, today, in the western world many people of all professions, classes, races and ages are questing for their greater Selves, for their true-life purpose, for authentic, life-positive spirituality. This is a spirituality which offers truthful orientation within the current chaos, which makes sense of the individual's meaning and which gives joy and fulfillment through the discovery of one's inherent gifts and potentials. Our deepest longing is to know who we really are, to experience our timeless, multidimensional being, to remember our spirit guides and often, also, to apply our connectedness to the benefit of others. We want to step out of the restricted, yet approved three-dimensional perception, and experience other realities in a safe way. LBL is a consciousness-expanding near-death and afterlife experience without any mortal danger, but with a deep-reaching healing effect and life-changing impact.

I am especially impressed by the author's integrity and modesty. She doesn't claim to offer the one truth, but the chance to find one's own truth, for example through the LBL experience. I am touched by her special way of describing the sensitivity and beauty of the human soul. The artful pictures share her love for this earthly life. The book has a directness and immediacy, as if while reading it you are having a talk with Rita, a woman with heart and wisdom.

To Soul Home and back ignites the memory of one's unique Soul, of being connected to other souls and other realms. All humans are longing for union with their "divine spark" – this timeless, multidimensional being of light, energy, consciousness and love. The soul is ignored by materialistic science and culture, and can be obstructed by formal religion. However, authentic memory and direct experience of this greater Self is essential for our awakening and evolving consciousness. It is the key to finding solutions for personal and collective problems, for co-creating a peaceful, loving world. It enables the balancing of dualistic poles: female and male, linear time and now-time, being and doing, loving others and loving oneself, "positive" and "negative" emotion.

The dark aspects of our planet can, in the long run, only be healed when they are accepted and integrated within by unconditional self-compassion and forgiving. They must be really loved so that they can be enlightened. However, the deepest fear in humans is not of darkness but of the powerful "Inner Divine", as Marianne Williamson so beautifully formulated, and Nelson Mandela cited. Therefore, a necessary step for humanity's healing is acknowledging the powerful liveliness, spontaneity and creativity of children from birth on, supporting their unique "divine spark". More souls than ever are incarnating to activate their Soul-consciousness, to share it with others and to finally bring "Heaven to Earth". Darkness is still fighting desperately for its survival, yet in parallel, the shadows on the planet lead evermore urgently towards compassion and love. LBL and this book contribute to that human evolution.

By **Peter Smith,**
Life Between Lives therapist,
President of The Michael Newton Institute
for Life Between Lives Hypnotherapy, Australia

There is a saying by John W. Gardner: "Some people make the world a better place, just by being the kind of people they are". Rita Borenstein is one of these people.

Some time back Rita told me she wanted to write a book about the work we do, called "Life Between Lives" Spiritual Regression. I was delighted and for good reason. While it takes great skill to facilitate the emergence of someone's immortal identity from the depths of their being into the light of understanding, in Rita we have something even more special ...

Some people do this work because they are inspired to offer it. Some people do it in the energy of service, and then there are some who do it for both these reasons and something more. For these people it is a calling, a deep and profound connection to their purpose for this lifetime – and that shines the brightest of all. This is what I see in Rita Borenstein, the author of the book you are about to read.

Life Between Lives (LBL) work is profound. This place where we go in between our incarnations is a place of peace, harmony and unconditional love. It has always been understood that at the time of our passing we reconnect with the greater spirituality of ourselves. Perhaps a Near Death Experience (NDE) can touch this also; however, those cases are usually accidental and occur without the assistance of an artful facilitator.

We take people "home" to their place of origin, to be with loving soul friends and in an energy that is hard to articulate in words. For me there can be no greater gift to another person, than to introduce them to their own soul. For the people who undertake this sacred journey, they are forever changed. They live life in conscious awareness of their immortality and not through belief in any religious doctrine, as it happens through absolute knowing from their own personal experience. It is no longer necessary to wait until the end of our life to touch your deepest authenticity and know our own soul; we can do it now and live the remainder of our days in an energy of immortal companionship.

This book is written in the gentle energy of selfless service, a beautiful echo of the loving way Rita offers LBL to the people who are drawn to her. A mixture of two stories – her own and one volunteer client who share his soul journeys with the world – are articulated with grace and skill. The stories are real, the people are real and the integration of the eternal learnings into this life carries inspiration for all of us.

The message to everyone is clear. Whether you are a surgeon or you have another station in life, all that is less relevant than the fact that you are a unique being, an individual expression of a greater consciousness. You are a spiritual being having a human experience, one designed by your own hand in the loving support of immortal beings who support your journey.

There is no greater message to everyone on this planet now. It offers a better understanding of our place in "all there is", a deeper perspective of life, and brings hope to those who need it most.

I know that as you read the pages that follow, your soul will feel the wisdom and the human aspect of your being will be renewed.

Dedication

I dedicate this book to Michael Newton Ph.D.

His legacy is the foundation of my daily work here in Sweden. Over many decades, and with seven thousand clients, he has documented, organized and created a method to take clients in deep hypnosis to the adventures of afterlife. With "Life Between Lives" LBL hypnotherapy for spiritual regression he has created opportunities for everybody who wants to get to know their identity, purpose and eternal theme of the soul.

Since I started to work with his method in 2013, many people have experienced his work by having sessions with me. I'd like to tell my story – how I found this method for deep soul research – as well as give my testimony based on my personal perception.

I use dialogues with a surgeon, as well as my own session, to show you examples of why and how an LBL can be meaningful for each person individually.

I have seen countless of clients awaken to the subjective truth that they incarnate many times, in many bodies, and never die as a soul identity. They tell me that this is how they grow and become wiser. Many awaken to their true life's mission, which adds a joy and happiness to them and their surroundings. They tell me that one single life, which is quite short, is not enough to develop as a soul. My belief is that when one person connects with the soul and heals from deep within, the relief and soulful beauty that radiates from that person spreads to their surroundings like ripples on water. This is a way in which each of us can heal ourselves and maybe even mend the world for generations coming after us.

Emerald Tablet –
Tabula Smaragdina

'Tis true without lying, certain & most true.

*That which is below is like that which is above
& that which is above is like that which is below
to do the miracles of one only thing.*

*And as all things have been & arose from one
by the mediation of one: so all things have their birth
from this one thing by adaptation.*

*The Sun is its father, the moon its mother, the wind hath
carried it in its belly, the earth is its nurse.*

The father of all perfection in the whole world is here.

Its force or power is entire if it be converted into earth.

*Separate thou the earth from the fire,
the subtle from the gross sweetly with great industry.*

*It ascends from the earth to the heaven & again
it descends to the earth & receives the force
of things superior & inferior.*

*By this means you shall have the glory of
the whole world & thereby all obscurity shall fly from you.*

*Its force is above all force. For it vanquishes every
subtle thing & penetrates every solid thing.*

So was the world created.

*From this are & do come admirable adaptations
whereof the means (or process) is here in this.
Hence I am called Hermes Trismegist, having
the three parts of the philosophy of the whole world
That which I have said of the operation of
the Sun is accomplished & ended.*

PART 1

Introduction

In search of my soul

Learning lessons is a little like reaching maturity.
You're not suddenly more happy, wealthy, or
powerful, but you understand the world around
you better, and you're at peace with yourself.
Learning life's lessons is not about
making your life perfect, but about seeing life
as it was meant to be.

Elisabeth Kübler-Ross

It is October 2012

I am in deep hypnosis in a huge mansion in the English countryside. Christine, a hypnotherapist from London, is sitting next to me. I am very relaxed and at the same time very alert.

We are attending a training arranged by The Newton Institute to learn how to facilitate Life Between Lives hypnotherapy for spiritual regression, based on the work and research of Michael Newton Ph.D.

We are all experienced hypnotherapists: a diverse group of head teachers, assistant teachers and students from India, Bosnia, the Netherlands, Norway, Italy, US, England, Vietnam, Romania, Taiwan, Australia, Denmark and Sweden.

I am deeply hypnotized

On April 15, 1945, British troops entered Bergen-Belsen. They liberated some 60,000 prisoners, many of whom were on the verge of death. During the first weeks after liberation, close to 500 people in Bergen-Belsen died every day. From liberation day until June 20, an estimated 14,000 people died from the terrible conditions that had been inflicted on them by the Nazis during the war.

In the following testimony, Judy Rosenzweig describes the liberation of Bergen-Belsen:

Suddenly out of the blue we saw tanks rolling into the camp ... We had no idea what kind of tanks they were. Is it the Americans? Is it the Germans? Is it ... we just didn't know. We became so panicked and at the same time the loudspeakers started speaking loudly in German and in English:

– You are liberated.

– We are the English Army – You are liberated.

– Stay away from danger and stay inside and we'll help you.

– Stay alive. Try to hang in there. We're here to help you.

With all my senses, I had a vivid experience of myself as an emaciated little girl about four years of age. When my hypnotherapist Christine asked me where I am, my answer is: "I am in a barrack in Bergen-Belsen."

It is cold and I am very weak. Deep in hypnosis, I have a clear bodily sensation that I am in a very dark place where my life is running out. Still, I am not afraid. It seems that I dissociate more and more. Soon I will leave my body behind in the barrack.

A man, of around thirty years old, who looks like a living skeleton, holds me in his arms as I leave my body, flying up, up and up. My tears are running down my cheeks as I feel the relief to finally be free. It is wonderful to leave the body in which I experienced this short life, after taking my last breath during horrible circumstances.

I feel the love flowing from the man who holds me in his arms when I die. Although he himself suffers and is probably close to his own death, he becomes bigger than himself and does not leave a child to die alone. His act of unconditional love is the last sensation I know before I die.

A loving meeting

Be at peace with your own soul, then heaven and earth will be at peace with you.

St. Rita De Cascia, born 1386 in Cascia, Italy. She is the patron saint of impossible causes, abuse victims and widows.

After I leave my tiny body behind on earth, I am ejected like from a catapult into space. I feel so free! It is a very strange and at the same time euphoric feeling to perceive myself without a physical body. Finally, free from inertia and limitations! The horrors down there do not affect me anymore, I was thinking. "Wow! I am free!" I scream out loud, and laugh for a while in my hypnotic state.

Then in my inner vision, I see a light in the distance. A beautiful and very feminine being is coming closer. I have this immense feeling of overwhelming joy and compassion radiating from the being that is approaching me. I tell Christine that my spirit guide has come to meet me! The being takes me to a place for rest and recreation. It feels wonderful! "Let's go to Soul Home!" she says.

It has been a very hard and short life, indeed! My guide tells me that I have been very brave. She invites me to talk about why I chose such a short and challenging life. Christine brings up a very important question: "What did you as a soul, learn from this short life, that you can use in your present life as Rita?"

I answer her that the man who showed me unconditional love before I left that life, is the reason I wanted to incarnate again. I wanted "to taste" that love again and meet this beautiful soul in "better conditions". Suddenly I just knew that the soul is one of my children this time. The insight filled my heart with deep joy. The feminine being then puts me in a love bath for restoration and rejuvenation.

Christine sits quietly and waits. Everything feels so real as I experience a passage in my first LBL.

Where is my ignition?

MY EVENING PRAYERS

Some time before I left for my LBL training in England, I had lost my igniting spark. I felt that nothing was fun anymore and perhaps I was depressed. One day, my brother gave me a drawing that I made as a child. When cleaning his drawers he found it and handed it over to me. At the bottom of the drawing it says: "An enclosed world" and it is signed by me, Rita Borenstein, nine years old.

My childhood drawing shows a very detailed garden filled with colourful flowers, growing vegetables and climbing plants. Some of the flowers seem to be enclosed by an aquarium like container. The drawing has a structure and the rows are very straight. The Finnish flag is in the front as I was born in Vaasa, Finland. But ... the beautiful garden is all fenced in, or maybe protected, by barbed wire.

In the upper part of the drawing there are two holes in the ground. One is inside and the other one is outside the fenced garden. Next to the outer hole lies a spade. It looks like somebody dug a hole to get out, left the spade on the ground and got out of the drawing. No person can be seen.

When I saw the quite strange drawing from my childhood, it was a reminder that my soul needed nutrition and my body was worn out. It was time to dig myself out again, symbolically and literally. I felt a longing, reaching up from the bottom of my soul, to find that spade again, to help myself to be free and blossom.

One night I decided to take a walk in the woods near our house outside Stockholm. While sitting on a stone covered with moss, I was wondering what to do next. Life felt so boring and I almost could not breathe. What should I do now? I suddenly heard an inner voice speak inside my head: "Pray and you shall receive!" So, I prayed for means to work with my gifts and skills for a higher good, to find the identity of my soul and to fulfil my life's purpose. I wanted badly my spark to ignite, so that I would become alive again.

I believe in magic

Behind the cotton wool is hidden a pattern;
that we – I mean all human beings—relate to this;
that the whole world is a work of art; that we are
parts of the work of art.

VIRGINIA WOOLF: MOMENTS OF BEING

Shortly after my prayers in the woods and just before the trip to my LBL training in England, I started to see number 4 increasingly often.

When I boarded the plane to England, I was offered seat number 44, the number of my hotel room in Manchester was 404. Next morning at breakfast I got table 44.

When the taxi arrived at the hotel, I saw the following written on the side of the car: Tiger Taxi 444 444.

As I noticed the synchronicity with the number 4, I felt that my spark had ignited again, so I gave the driver a big smile and jumped into the back seat.

I felt happy, excited and alive. I felt that destiny had taken me by the hand. It was like going home to the Promised Land, although still not knowing what that exactly meant.

~

What is Life Between Lives (LBL) Hypnotherapy for Spiritual Regression?

~

*Spiritual perception must be an individual quest
or it has no meaning. We are greatly
influenced by our own immediate reality,
and we can act on that reality one step at a time
without the necessity of seeing too far into
the distance. Even steps in the wrong direction give
us insight into the many paths designed to teach us.
To bring the soul Self into harmony with
our physical environment, we are given freedom of
choice to exercise free will in the search
for the reasons why we are here.
On the road of life, we must take responsibility
for all our decisions without blaming other people
for life's setbacks that bring unhappiness.*

DR. MICHAEL NEWTON: *DESTINY OF SOULS
– NEW CASE STUDIES OF LIFE BETWEEN LIVES*

I can feel my soul identity, living through aeons of time, changing bodies like costumes when they wear out. Who would I be today if I remembered the essence of what I learned from all those lives?

In 2012, I longed to get to the bones of things and figure out my life mission. One day after my prayers in the woods, I found the books by Dr. Michael Newton. I had bought his books back in the 90's. Through many decades of work, and with seven thousand clients, Dr. Newton found that it was possible not only to regress to a past life in hypnosis, but also to the nonphysical experience between lives.

I met people who had near-death experiences (NDE) and was amazed by their stories. The interlife hypnosis that Dr. Newton described, was the closest I could come to experience an NDE in an organized and safe way together with a person trained in hypnotherapy to assist me.

The book *Journey of Souls* totally resonated with me and what I had felt to be my own truth about my eternal soul. I was curious of the method that Dr. Newton had created and written about, so I decided to experience LBL hypnosis. My search for someone trained in this regression method opened the door to becoming the first Life Between Lives facilitator in Sweden. I was accepted as a student at The Newton Institute (TNI) training in October 2012.

During the training, I had my first LBL, which revolution-
ized my belief system and way of living. My true purpose in
life became clearer to me and I felt my deeper identity as a
soul.

The first LBL facilitator in Sweden

Cherish your visions and your dreams
as they are the children of your soul, the blueprints
of your ultimate achievements.

Napoleon Hill

When I was young, I took care of all sorts of displaced animals. My best friend as a child was the journalist Mrs. Marianne Vainio. I still remember that she introduced me to the books written by the philosopher Krishnamurti. We spent a lot of time together. I learned much from her about life, especially from her kindness to all living creatures. We shared the passion for animals.

When it was time to choose a profession, all I could imagine was becoming a nurse. My plan was to be economically independent quickly and move as far away as possible from my hometown. As in my childhood drawing, where I was digging myself out of the fenced garden, I longed to go out into the world with a great purpose of some sort. What that great purpose was all about, was hard to tell, but I thought becoming a nurse would be a good start. Since early childhood I longed to be of use, somehow, for a higher good.

It is a very interesting work to facilitate LBL sessions for many kinds of characters and personalities. Since my training, I have worked passionately with clients arriving at my practice from all parts of Sweden. I use all my natural skills and gifts in this work, which is very fulfilling and stimulating. My life's training from twenty years of professional nursing and another twenty years as a Chinese Medicine Acupuncture practitioner and Osteopath D.O. trained in Biodynamic Cranial Osteopathy, as well as the former owner of Center for Wellbeing, a holistic center in Stockholm, all added up and led to becoming an LBL facilitator by the age of 56, the last two numbers of the year in which I was born.

I estimate that about 90% of my clients have read one or all of Michael Newton's three books; *Journey of Souls, Destiny of Souls* and *Life Between Lives Hypnotherapy for Spiritual Regression*. Many have also read *Memories of Afterlife,* a collection of LBL case studies written by members of The Newton Institute, each story commented by Dr. Newton. In 2016, The Newton Institute created *Stories of Afterlife*, which is an online newsletter including new case studies and news from TNI.

Many seek their life's true mission and soul identity. Some

of them long for changes in their lives. Others want to release their feeling of stagnation. Some tell me that they were deeply touched by the books of Dr. Newton and feel a calling to contact me for a session to see for themselves.

After my own first LBL, my work as a therapist was over. To be an LBL facilitator is something quite different. Instead of focusing on the health, sickness and wellbeing of the client, I became someone who facilitates their own search for existential deep truth, healing and meaning. I see clients who, just like me in 2012, want to go deeper into themselves.

The hosting body versus soul

Dogmas or systems of thought that tell you
to rise above your emotions can be misleading –
even, in your terms, somehow dangerous.
Such theories are based upon the concept that there
is something innately disruptive, base,
or wrong in man's emotional nature,
while the soul is always depicted as being calm,
"perfect", passive and unfeeling.
Only the most lofty, blissful awareness is allowed.
Yet the soul is above all a fountain of energy,
creativity, and action that shows its characteristics
in life precisely through the ever-changing emotions.

JANE ROBERTS: *THE NATURE OF PERSONAL REALITY*

Dr. Newton calls the body the "hosting body" meaning the "package" or the "costume" we travel in during a life. The soul is the eternal identity that enters the new hosting body at a certain time before birth and leaves at death.

If possible I ask my LBL clients when their soul entered the fetus during the time in the womb of their mother. Some clients say they entered in the beginning, some in the middle and some closer to birth. It is always interesting to hear the explanation why their soul entered at a special moment during the development of the new hosting body. Dr. Newton noticed, based on thousands of cases, that it takes time for the soul and the new hosting body to adjust to each other during the time in the womb of the mother.

If possible, I also ask why the client choose the particular time and place to be born. Many clients tell me a lot about their choice of mother and father, hosting body, their soul connection and other things. It is amazing what the client reports when deeply regressed to the very beginning of their life as a fetus just before birth.

I'd like to share a memory from one regression to the womb of the mother with a client. The reason for this client coming for his LBL session, was to find out why he always felt such sadness and loneliness even together with other people. He told me while in deep trance, that he did not feel alone in the womb of the mother. Then he had a dialogue with his (identical) twin brother, who told him that it was planned for them to be born together and for him to become disabled, sent away to an orphanage and then die alone as four years old without his family. When my client unexpectedly met his twin brother in the womb experience, they talked about deeply important things that helped the client understand himself better.

A few weeks after his LBL experience, the client called me. He told me that after the session, he made a research and found his brother's files from the orphanage. His brother had been left there right after their birth and died by the age of four, just as the client was told by his twin brother during his session. My client had told me before the session that although he felt such deep sadness, he had never cried. During the conversation in hypnosis with his twin brother, I remember that he cried a lot. So did I, actually, I was very moved. He told me that his experience in the LBL helped him heal his long standing deep sadness.

The eternal existential questions

*Our eternal identity never leaves us alone
in the bodies we choose, despite our status.
In reflexion, meditation, or prayer,
the memories of who we really are
do filter down to us in selective thought each day.
In small, intuitive ways – through
the cloud of amnesia – we are given clues
for the justification of our being.*

Michael Newton Ph.D.

When life is going well, day after day, existential questions do not pop up that often. But in times of challenges, for example when we become ill or lose a loved one, this kind of questions arise in all of us when we feel unhappy, bored or stagnant. We might ask ourselves, especially when we get older, if there is no more to life than this.

My sincere wish is to introduce you to a method by which your own existential questions can be answered. Before an LBL, my clients list their questions and send them to me. During the LBL I will ask my client those questions along the way, so they will be answered by their own inner soul Self. There is a saying that you hear something "straight from the horse's mouth", meaning that it comes from the highest authority. This is the case here, because the information comes from the client and not from someone else.

An LBL, which usually takes three to five hours, includes being regressed to childhood, inside the womb of the mother, and to a past life. From the past life, the client crosses over in a death scene and then travels to the afterlife from there. That is when the so called Life Between Lives journey starts.

About hypnosis

You use hypnosis not as a cure but as a means of establishing a favorable climate in which to learn.

Milton Erickson

The history of hypnosis goes back to temple sleep in ancient Greece and Egypt. Sleep temples, also known as dream temples, are regarded as places where hypnosis took place over 4,000 years ago under the influence of Imhotep who served as Chancellor and High Priest of the sun god Ra at Heliopolis. Sleep temples were hospitals of sorts, healing a variety of ailments, perhaps many of them psychological in nature. The treatment involved chanting, placing the patient into a trancelike or hypnotic state and analyzing their dreams in order to determine treatment. Meditation, fasting, baths and sacrifices to the patron deity or other spirits were often involved.

Sleep temples also existed in the Middle East and Ancient Greece. In Greece, they were built in honor of Asclepius, the Greek god of medicine. The Greek treatment was referred to as incubation and focused on prayers to Asclepius for healing.

Avicenna (Ibn Sina) (980–1037), a Persian psychologist and physician, was the earliest to make a distinction between sleep and hypnosis. In "The Book of Healing", which he published in 1027, he referred to hypnosis in Arabic as al-Wahm al-Amil, stating that one could create conditions in another person so that he/she accepts the reality of hypnosis.

The modern era of hypnosis and hypnotherapy really begins with Franz Anton Mesmer (1734-1815), the Viennese physician who left the word "mesmerism" to posterity. For various reasons, he also gave hypnosis the rather bad reputation that still persists in some quarters today.

Some of my clients have seen stage hypnosis on TV and think that the whole thing is somewhat scary. But after we have gone through all the preparations on the phone and email, when they arrive and have a talk before we start the session, they usually feel relaxed and ready to start the hypnosis. After all, hypnosis is only a state of deep relaxation and a way to get in touch with oneself.

A neurological explanation to hypnosis is the theory of different brain waves and their reciprocality to mental states. Brain waves are divided into five categories of progressively higher frequencies (expressed in Hertz, Hz or cycles per second):

- Delta 0-4Hz sleep state

- Theta 4-8 Hz deep trance state

- Alpha 8-12Hz hypnagogic states, meditation, hypnosis

- Beta 12-25 Hz awake state

- Gamma 25-100+Hz feeling of being in "flow" or "in the zone", state of peak performance

Theta deep trance state is favorable to access deep seated soul memories in LBL.

My clients in hypnosis focus on my voice and are attentive, but at the same time their bodies are so relaxed that they hardly move during all the hours of their LBL. When they are invited to answer my questions, the magical moment starts when they speak their inner truth in their relaxed hypnotic state. What they say seems wiser and more filled with reflection than their ordinary way of speaking. The deeper they go into hypnosis, the more memories on a soul level they seem to remember.

Some of the clients are visually oriented and see pictures and "inner movies" during the hypnosis. Others perceive in other ways, led by inner knowing, hearing or feeling. All of us are unique, so our inner senses work differently and individually while hypnotized as well.

In a hypnotic state, we can relive moments and feel fear, joy, anger and other feelings. It is also possible to "watch" these moments from outside, and report about them, as with the voice of a narrator. These phenomena may alter during the session. Here is an example of this kind of dual awareness with my client, the so called "Surgeon". In a passage of his past life experience as the soldier Ray, he talks about a moment when he is mortally wounded. When I ask him to look at his wounds from the perspective of the experienced surgeon, he alternates to another perspective and watches his body from outside.

Rita: So, what happens now, Ray?

Surgeon: *I have a lot of bullets in my abdomen.*

R: Do you die right away from this?

S: *No. It feels as if the whole right part of me is wounded.*

R: Can you look a little closer?

S: (Sighs.) *Let me look! It feels like my right leg below the knee is hanging like a ragdoll. It looks as if it exploded in some way and is now totally shattered. I have bullets in my abdomen, and it feels like I have bullets that have penetrated right through my back also. Then there is something with my right hand, but I can't see that now. I will not live much longer. I feel neither sad nor in physical pain.*

R: What causes your death?

S: *I am bleeding somewhere in the abdomen, but I do not bleed a lot. That is strange. It feels like I will manage for a couple of hours. I am lying alone.*

R: Can you please use your knowledge as a surgeon now and give me a diagnosis of the medical state of Ray?

S: *When I look at myself from the outside, I notice many bullet wounds in the abdomen that have not taken the blood vessels, so there are intestines that are wounded. I also have my legs all shattered by bullets, well partly, but those blood vessels are in cramp, so they do not bleed anymore, and I do not bleed to death. In the same way, I have a few injuries in my arms, the right one ... and why just on the right side, I do not know. All this is not going to make me die right away, but I will die soon, within a day maximum.*

R: What time of the day is it now?

S: *It feels like night, and I am lying here looking. I know that I am going to die. I cannot end it, but will just have to wait. I am not afraid!*

R: Ray, thank you for reporting all this to me now!

Many of my clients have no experience of hypnosis, while some have had several sessions before with me or someone else. The clients who have no experience from hypnosis before, often need to do at least one preparatory session before their LBL, to find out how this kind of deep and long hypnosis works for them. Nobody can tell another person what hypnosis feels like, because we all have a unique way to experience relaxation and inner knowing. The preparatory session is important for me as well, because I need to know if my client can go as deep as remembering a past life which is the key to go to the LBL state. According to the findings of Dr. Newton's research we most naturally enter the LBL state through the death moment and crossing over from a past life.

I would also like to mention that I do not take clients into any kind of hypnosis who seem emotionally and mentally unstable, are drug addicts or are diagnosed mentally or severely physically ill.

The perspective of time

There is "clock time" and there is "happy time". Additionally, there is "hypnotic time". In our daily lives, "clock time" is the common pacemaker in the western world. By "happy time", I mean the moments that pass by unnoticed when feeling truly happy, losing ourselves in something we enjoy or being with someone we love. When we are bored, time moves slowly and when we are enjoying the moment, time flies. This we all know.

Hypnosis is very much like "happy time", but even more relaxing and amusing. When a person is in a deep hypnotic state, most often he/she feels deeply focused, moved, amused, excited and enjoys the moment. At the same time, there is no sense of the passing of time, so the experience is bathed in a sense of wonder. I think it is great that we humans can relax deeply and go into hypnagogic states. A huge benefit is that during LBL hypnosis we access the deeper soul memories that we do not naturally remember in daily life. My experience is also that hypnosis in general, and LBL in particular, is a very healing experience on all levels, even the physical.

The preparation for an LBL

Our soul may be travelling away from a permanent home, but we are not just tourists. We bear responsibility in the evolution of a higher consciousness for ourselves and others in life. Thus, our journey is a collective one.

Michael Newton Ph.D.

To prepare well before an LBL is very important. After the initial contact I give the client instructions how to prepare for the session. If the preparation is done well, the session will be more fulfilling.

After the initial interview as the session begins, I go into a light meditative, relaxed state of inner stillness. It is my way to stay in tune with my client and provide support and encouragement in a loving and relaxed way.

During an LBL session, the client goes progressively deeper into relaxation over the three to four hours ahead from beginning to end. The client often arrives at my practice a little nervous and excited. As we start talking and have a cup of tea in my kitchen, they become more relaxed. I encourage the client to feel free to let me know how they feel.

Once the real session starts and when my client has become very relaxed and shows signs of hypnosis, we start the "warming up" as Dr. Newton called his technique, to prepare the client for deep theta brainwave hypnosis. "The warming up" is a regression to childhood and then to the time in the mother's womb just before birth. Later, the client is invited to go to a past life, if possible.

When the session really starts to kick off and the client's inner knowing becomes clear, it is very similar to sitting in a movie theatre and to become so fascinated by the story that you forget about yourself. You just go with the flow and enjoy.

The most common questions I hear from new clients are:

1. *Will hypnosis work for me?*

2. *Can I go to the toilet if I need to during all these hours?*

3. *Do I sleep when hypnotized?*

4. *What if I never wake up?*

My answers:

1. The only way to know is to try it out! What is needed is to be able to relax, to focus on the moment and to trust the process. When it works, it feels like our souls dance together in harmony. Some people have gone through difficult

things and do not trust or open themselves even if they want to. Because I am also a trained therapist, I usually suggest other healing modalities or a few preparatory sessions that hopefully will assist my client.

2. Yes.

3. Hypnosis is a state of awake relaxation, not the same as sleep. If the client falls asleep during the session it can be a sign of psychological protection or that their nervous system just tells them about their lack of sleep.

4. There are many horror stories about hypnosis and the risk of falling asleep and not waking up is one of them. Most of my clients rather do the opposite: they come out of the hypnosis spontaneously if there is something that bothers them.

Every person has a name

*Now your physical body is a field of energy
with a certain form. However, and when someone
asks you your name, your lips speak it – and yet
the name does not belong to the atoms
and molecules in the lips that utter the syllables.
The name has meaning only to you.
Within your body you cannot put your finger
upon your own identity. If you could travel
within your body, you could not find
where your identity resides, yet you say,
"This is my body," and, "This is my name."*

Jane Roberts: *Seth speaks*

– The eternal validity of the soul

During all sessions, it is important to avoid entity confusion. That is why I continually ask the questions: "Who are you now and what is your name now?" I want to know who I am talking with.

Of course, the name of my client is important, but as the session proceeds, there will be many more names. When the client descends into childhood, the names of parents, siblings, relatives and friends are important to them, and I need to write them down in case the client mentions the name later in the session. When the client goes to a past life, I ask them about their past life name and the names of people they find important there and then. When they go to afterlife they often remember their soul name, their Guide's name, and the names and soul names of those in their soul group. That is a lot of names. Some names are often difficult to memorize, because I never heard names before like "Vairy" or "Avron".

We all receive a name when we are born. A name is often associated with the energy and radiance the person has. If you have a name you are somebody. Prisoners in concentration camps had numbers tattooed on their arms, because they were reduced to a number, and the name was considered irrelevant. By taking away the name and other personal attributes, like hair and clothes, humans have treated each other with disrespect and cruelty.

The Guide

Our spiritual teachers have different styles and
techniques, just like teachers on Earth.
Their immortal characters have been matched
to our own essence in a variety of ways.

Dr. Michael Newton

Dr. Newton discovered, based on the consistent responses of 7,000 clients, that we all seem to have a "Primary Guide". I heard stories from clients who felt a presence in a life-threatening situation, like an accident or severe illness. Many of my LBL clients connect with their Primary Guide during the LBL session.

From the moment when the client has crossed over from a past life, the Guide most often meets the homecoming soul. An example of this is the feminine being who came to me after dying as a child in Bergen-Belsen. After my client connected with his or her Guide I ask questions like: "Where does your Guide want to take you now" or "ask your Guide what is important now" etc. In this stage my role is not so prominent.

Soul group, cluster group

When clients tell me how much they suffered
from the actions of family members,
my first question to their conscious mind is,
"If you had not been exposed
to this person as a child,
what would you
now lack in understanding?"
It may take a while,
but the answer is in our minds.
There are spiritual reasons for our
being raised as children around certain
kinds of people, just as other people are designated
to be near us as adults.

Dr. Michael Newton: *Journey of Souls*

– Case Studies of Life Between Lives

Dr. Newton's theory is that in each life we travel with a cast of characters, just like in a screenplay or a film. We share our lives with people with and from whom we learn our life lessons. Some of these people we experience as comforting and loving, while others cause us constant struggle. There are people we recognize right away in a so called "déjà vu" (seen before) and maybe even fall in love with at first sight. There are people we hate at first sight too, even though we do not know them.

Before an LBL, the client gives me a list of their significant people. While the client is in deep trance we try to figure out more about these people/souls on a deeper level. During an LBL hypnosis, it is possible to remember all sorts of connections on the soul level and this often explains a lot of things for the client. It is also possible to bring clarity to the connections within a family and extended family, or between friends, children, parents and lovers.

Station stops

The gardens may flow with beauty
But let us go to the Gardener Himself.

Jalal ad-Din Muhammad Rumi

The most common station stops are the Library, the Classroom, the Garden or the Temple. Clients often give their own names to these places. I still remember a client who met her soul group in a bar. I have also heard clients describe many other places resembling places on earth.

One can look at these station stops as metaphorical places: a library symbolizing a search for information; a classroom as a place for learning; a garden as a place for recreation and reflection and a temple as a place for worship and meeting with divine wisdom. A bar might symbolize the thirst for spirit. The word "spirit" then has dual meaning: to seek spirit in a bottle or searching within in other spiritual ways. During the LBL, these places are described very vividly by my clients. Through their eyes, I can follow them to these magical station stops where I ask the client their own questions when appropriate.

Dr. Newton gives an explanation based on his research why clients experience rooms, places, people and circumstances so like earthly conditions. He says that all souls have their individual way of projecting meaningful pictures and symbols that reconnect to their physical reality even after death. For example, I had a client who was a writer and considered the written word as her main interest in life. As soon as she came to the Soul Home in her LBL, she went to a huge library where she could talk with a librarian and ask questions.

Going to a place of higher learning

When one has been born and has died many times,
expecting extinction with each death,
and when this experience is followed
by the realization that existence still continues,
then a sense of the divine comedy enters in.

JANE ROBERTS: *SETH SPEAKS*

– THE ETERNAL VALIDITY OF THE SOUL

A very fascinating part of the LBL is when my client goes to "a place of higher learning". Each client seems to have their own name for the place where they meet with wise beings. This is a phase in the LBL where all the important questions of the client can be brought up again and, if possible, answered by these wise beings.

In my own LBL, I came into a giant hall of white marble, where I met my "Council of Elders". I entered the temple with my Guide. There were seven old men dressed in white clothing like in ancient Greece. They were standing in a semicircle and seemed to invite me closer, telling me not to be afraid. I felt very humble and slowly got closer. Soon enough the leader of the Council told me that my meeting with them was to start. My Guide was standing behind me. As I got closer it was possible to describe their features, their dresses and a lot of details to my LBL facilitator, Christine.

I felt that my arrival was expected and that these seven men knew more about me and my soul journey than I did myself. One of the most important and urgent questions was about my future professional path. I wondered if becoming an LBL facilitator was right for me, or whether I should continue working as an Osteopath and healer, or maybe do something quite different.

As the meeting with my Council began, the leader, who radiated an infinite wisdom and kindness, indicated that all the Council members would vote about how to answer my question. Suddenly, each of all the members were holding a large placard. From left to right, one by one showed me their placard, saying "Yes" (meaning only LBL work from now on) or "No" (meaning work with something else). It turned out that five votes were "Yes", one was "No" and the last was "let Rita decide".

This illustrates the wisdom of "free choice". Most of the Council gave me a hint and a recommendation, while the seventh member reminded me of free will and to follow my heart. It takes courage to make a choice. They probably knew that I had already made up my mind to work with LBL and was asking just to be sure. My meeting with them was very reassuring and I was happy for their unconditional love and support.

Different kinds of souls

*Success consists of going from failure to failure
without loss of enthusiasm.*

Winston Churchill

When clients go deep into hypnosis they usually tell me about their advancement as souls over aeons of time. Some of my clients seem to struggle in their current life with similar or the same issues and themes as they have done over many, many lives.

To stand up for oneself, to overcome fear or to fight and die in war are examples of such themes. In our mundane lives, we stumble over a solution, get up and keep going in the same way, with the same outcome. The spiritual leader Eckhart Tolle says: "If you think you are so spiritual, go spend a weekend with your parents". By this he probably means that there are many who say: "I have worked with myself all my life", and yet still feel a lot of anger and resentment with their parents. But if you choose these parents and life conditions on a soul level, why blame them?

Dr. Newton made a classification model for soul development levels. In *Journey of Souls* he tells us about what he calls

Beginner Souls, Intermediate Souls and Advanced Souls.

He based his classification on the colours that his 7,000 clients reported.

Level 1: Beginner, white, off-white and reddish pink

Level 2: Lower intermediate, white and reddish pink, light orange with tints of white

Level 3: Intermediate, yellow, deep gold with tints of green

Level 4: Upper intermediate, green or brownish green

Level 5: Advanced, light blue, light blue with gold, green or brown tints, deep blue

Level 6: Highly advanced, deep blue with tints of purple

Higher Levels: Purple

Michael Newton Ph.D.: *Life between Lives hypnotherapy for Spiritual Regression. Appendix page 216*
Dr. Newton wrote that almost three-quarters of all souls who inhabit human bodies on earth today are still in the early stages of development. He writes about this in *Journey of Souls* and I quote him: "I know this is a grossly discouraging statement because it means most of our human population is operating at the lower end of their training".

A characteristic of a beginner soul is a person who goes

through daily life without reflection and learning from mistakes or experience. A Beginner Soul can be extremely vulnerable – like a small child who is not experienced in handling life.

The Intermediate Soul have acquired the maturity and experience for operating more independently.

Having mastered the fundamental issues most of us wrestle with daily, the Advanced Soul is more interested in making small refinements towards specific tasks. An Advanced Soul is recognized by their kind and wise appearance. Some of them look transparent to me, because they radiate total love and acceptance. They seem to have nothing to hide. They are not necessarily the ones who speak the loudest and often stay in the background.

There are souls that specialize in teaching, healing, animal protection, environmental and many other areas where the soul incarnates again and again to work and develop skills in. Knowing that I myself am a healer soul, emanating the colour green, gives me great pleasure to fulfil my destiny with the work I do. It is important for me to take full responsibility for my own needs and live out the saying: "healer, heal thyself!" Over the years, I have seen many examples of health professionals and healers who help others, but do not help themselves. To heal oneself can be more difficult than helping others. Facing my own darkness and shadows is necessary to prevent me from projecting it out on others.

Here is what the hypnotized Surgeon is telling me about his soul advancement:

Rita: How advanced is your soul Vairy?

Surgeon: *The feeling I have is that I am rather advanced. I mean that if you are standing looking down, there are lots below and if you are looking up, there are lots above.*

R: What is the reason for you, as a soul, to incarnate?

S: *I have come a long way. I do not have to descend to earth to learn so much more. That is my feeling. I am quite done with it. There was no joy, there was no sadness. It was a mission meant to be* (meaning his life as the soldier Ray). *But I did not get any wiser from it, nor dumber either, for that matter.*

Time to incarnate again,
choice of body

The meaning of incarnate is precisely what its Latin roots suggest. The prefix in- means "in" and caro means "flesh," so incarnate means "in the flesh."

Just before the long and adventurous LBL journey comes to an end, we try to figure out why and how the client chose the current body. The question is – if we, on a soul level, have the possibility to choose the body we are in now – then why this specific one?

If we have lived a life with a lot of struggle, we might not want to believe that we choose that life consciously. I remember a client who told me that her choice of body had meant a very difficult life for her. When I asked her when hypnotized why she choose a difficult life, she said that it gave her a fantastic opportunity to learn a lot and develop. An easy life is not the best way, she said, but is sometimes needed in certain circumstances just to rest.

To come back after an LBL hypnosis

Feeling my way through the darkness
Guided by a beating heart
I can't tell where the journey will end
But I know where to start
They tell me I'm too young to understand
They say I'm caught up in a dream
Well life will pass me by if I don't open up my eyes
Well that's fine by me
So wake me up when it's all over
When I'm wiser and I'm older
All this time I was finding myself, and I
Didn't know I was lost

Avicii, Tim Bergling 1989-2018

Clients in hypnosis have no sense of time. When I slowly bring them back to the present, they are always surprised that three to five hours have passed. The client goes into the core of their being and navigates there for many hours together with me. It is obvious that the return to the here and now must be slow and comfortable.

When the client starts to come back to a waking state, they are often overwhelmed by their experience. Before they come back completely, I usually take them to a guided grounding meditation, a long silence and rest to help them integrate and heal.

It is important to let the client have their own moments in peace. Some clients signal that they want to share and talk about what they just had experienced. Then I am open to listen, but do not encourage them to speak. Silence is very good at this stage.

When it is all happily over, we have a snack or a cup of tea. After all, we have travelled together and navigated in their Soul Home for many hours. This is of course an unusual thing to do with a complete stranger – which we were before the session began. When we say goodbye I always have a feeling that destiny made our paths cross at a specific moment in time. Shortly after they left my house I notice the same phenomena similar to when I wake up after a dream. I remember it all clearly at first, but very quickly it fades away. So, I am never personally burdened by any of these sessions. On the contrary I feel that somehow I was healed as well every time. I learned a saying during my training to become an Osteopath D.O. It goes: " Find it, fix it and leave it alone."

~

My second LBL session

~

A past life as Dr. Helen in Vienna

But humans are forgetful animals. We forget that we have a story beyond our current circumstances, that we may have come into this world with an assignment and an identity that predates our present lives and won't end when our present bodies are left behind. Forgetting who we are, and what our soul purpose is in the world, we get into all kinds of trouble. The situation gets worse when we lose some of our vital essence because things happen to us and part of us wants to check out of the body and may actually succeed, a condition that shamans call soul loss and shrinks call dissociation.

Robert Moss: *Dreaming the Soul Back Home*

– Shamanic Dreaming for Healing and Becoming Whole.

Becoming the first LBL facilitator in Sweden in 2013 made my practice very busy. After a year I felt a longing to see an LBL colleague for a second LBL. I travelled to England to have a session with my TNI mentor.

This time I experienced a past life as a woman, named Helen. She lived and worked in Vienna during the end of the 19th and beginning of the 20th century. She was totally devoted to her calling as an obstetrician delivering children at a time when the death of both mother and child was very common.

When she was young, she loved witty dialogues and quick dances. But as she got older, she started to wither away from working too much. She lived alone and had no children. Gradually she became a very lonely "workaholic". She died in a bed in the same hospital where she spent most of her life working.

In my present life, I see myself in her. What Helen and I have in common is a passion for what we believe in. We both tend to work hard, without taking time to rest and care for our physical needs. Working a lot can often be a way to escape life, just like too much drinking, eating, shopping and other ways that slowly take over so we lose control. My great challenge today is to change this kind of addictive pattern.

In 1850, Dr. Semmelweis saved lives with three words: "Wash your hands!" Before the existence of bacteria was common knowledge, he realized that death in childbirth could be reduced if doctors washed their hands after surgical operations and before touching the birth canals of mothers giving birth. I can imagine how it might have been to work as a female doctor in Vienna in the aftermath of Dr. Semmelweis. He was a very controversial medical doctor, ridiculed and died alone and forgotten in an asylum for mentally disturbed people.

When I was deeply hypnotized I felt that I was Helen completely and wholeheartedly. In that way, I could "relive" that past life and bring out the essence of what I learned. In what follows, Helen is speaking about herself through me when I was deeply hypnotized.

LBL facilitator: Go back in time to your recent past life or another important life! Where are you now? Tell me!

Rita: *I am in Vienna! I have the feeling of being with all these intellectuals and artists. I am a woman in a group. I am twenty years old.*

L: Please tell me how you are dressed!

R: *The shoes I wear have heels, and one of those straps that hold the shoe in place. I wear black, rather thick stockings and skirt. The skirt has layer upon layer and go down to my ankles. I have a very thin waist. My hair is long and set in a kind of hair-do. Many pins keep it in place. I am not poor. In some way, I have the freedom to do what I want. Maybe I am a daughter of someone with money?*

L: Tell me more about yourself!

R: *Oh, this is such a fun life! And yes, I feel very beautiful. All men look at me! It feels good, but I also have a few talents that make them notice me. I do not know what I do – but I do something. It is the beginning of 1900 and there is something exciting about the new century. In our group, we engage in intellectual fellowship; we throw intelligent comments at each other back and forth. Things are not moving that fast. Everything takes its time – and we have fun as we are doing it. I like to dance fast. I love the quick dances* (laughing). *We dance a kind of quick one that goes around and round. My body is quick and I love to dance!*

L: Sounds wonderful! Please tell me more about the circumstances!

R: *We all study different things. All subjects are interlinked in some way, so we feel that we study aspects of the same thing. I have a feeling now that I study medicine. It is not that common for a woman. I also have a feeling of walking around in a hospital.*

L: What is your name?

R: *My name is Helen! Helen something ... Helen ... I have a feeling that I am a Jewess. My family name is somewhat Jewish ...*

Yes, I am a doctor. I am about forty and I am very serious now. I do not dance that often. It is something about being a woman and helping others in a way that male doctors cannot. I work very hard. And there are so many people with female diseases and related conditions. I understand them somehow. I get a feeling now that it is about childbirth mostly. I have some kind of speciality. Yes I know now that I am an obstetrician.

L: Do you have any children of your own, Helen?

R: *No, I do not have any children. I think I am in love with someone, but I do not have that family feeling at all. Yes, I devote myself completely to my work. It would not be possible for me to work and have children. It is like a decision. Or it just does not happen that I care to have a family of my own. I am in love with someone. But I work so hard and I am always so tired in the evening and then I think ... I have no energy to do anything about it.*

L: Thank you for telling me all this Helen! Can you describe a bit more what your daily life is like?

R: *I need all the energy, because it is very demanding. The midwives take care of the childbirths, but they call me when there are complications. I get to deal with the difficult cases. And I do home calls and the situations are sometimes so weird* *and ... Now I feel that my voice changes ... when I become Helen. I am very grounded. Because I must be, otherwise I cannot ... but I just work and then I return home ... and I work ... and I use all my energy for this.*

L: Sounds like very hard work, Helen! How do you manage?

R: *Yes, I can only trust my skills, because there is no other help at hand. And the baby needs to come out and I must calculate the situation. I stay with the mother all the time to monitor and to see that all goes well. There are a few tricks that I know from experience, for example how to turn the baby inside the womb and how to treat the mother when it is done. And, as I am a woman myself, I can have a better feel for it, even though I never gave birth myself. The woman relaxes more with a female doctor. So, in one way or another, I manage to save a lot of children from dying and I also save the lives of the mothers.*

L: Can you help me understand by explaining more in detail how you work?

R: *First, the birth must go in stages. And it must be synchronized with the rhythm of the mother and that is what I am a specialist in. In a way, it is my speciality to know the general rhythm of the procedure and that is why I manage to save so many children. I never rush and I never pull the baby out un-*

less necessary. I know that the mother will push her baby out at exactly the right moment. I just encourage and help the baby out, of course, but I do not use any violence.

L: What is your driving force, Helen? What is in this for you?

R: *I also feel very satisfied, because this is exactly what I want to do. And when a child is born and I know the mother is well and the child is fine, that also gives me immense joy.*

L: Helen tell me, is there anybody in your life you feel close to?

R: *The most important person is Fritz, an older doctor here in the hospital. We admire each other, one could say. I feel that he is quite influential where I work. He helps me out in situations when people do not believe in me, and circumstances like that. While I am generally self-confident, it is sometimes hard with the other male doctors. Fritz helps me out very often. There is love between us, but we are not in love in that way. He is a comfortable friend and a great supporter. I can discuss difficult cases with him. I believe he is the only person Helen feels close to or the only important one. He is like a father figure.*

L: Can we continue now to a time in your life, Helen, when you are older?

R: *Yes. Now I am older! When I grow older as Helen I do not care as much about the group of intellectual fellowship. They were fun to be with, but we were not that close. I am so grounded now and so busy. I do not have time to run around! I am very ambitious in my profession. I want to save lives! I am also curious about developments in the medical field. Things do not advance fast; there is a lot of superstition about things, especially childbirths, that cause many to lose their children. They do not know how to handle things. It is all rather primitive. It upsets me.*

L: I understand. Must be hard for you! How do you feel about your own body Helen?

R: *I feel that my stiffness is increasing, the older I become. I feel like an old maid because I have no sexuality. I can feel that my body has no physical stimulus, no sex, no tactile stimulation, just layers and layers of responsibility. I become dryer and dryer, skinnier and skinnier.*

Last day and Helen's death

Trusted, your feelings will lead you to psychological and spiritual states of mystic understanding, calm, and peacefulness. Followed, your emotions will lead you to deep understandings, but you cannot have a physical self without emotions any more than you can have a day without weather.

JANE ROBERTS: *THE NATURE OF PERSONAL REALITY*

In deep hypnosis, I am now coming closer to the day of my death in my life as Dr. Helen. At this point I felt so physically weak that I had to whisper my answers to my LBL facilitator. That is how authentic my experience in hypnosis was!

LBL facilitator: So please tell me what is going on right now Helen! How do you feel?

Rita: *I feel so weak, because I have worked so much. I am in a hospital bed and Fritz has died. After his death, I feel no enthusiasm. I am not that old yet, but I feel completely worn out. I am not happy, I am not unhappy, I just feel: "That was that". I am in a bed in the hospital where I used to work. The nurses* *are very nice to me. There are no relatives here with me, just the nurses.*

L: You are a very good doctor, so would you like to tell me more about your medical condition right now Helen?

R: *It is something with my breathing – lung disease. That is why I have become so skinny. But I do not know why I have a problem with my lungs. I feel that my voice is like a soufflé that sinks.* (Whispers.) *I can only speak like this. Very low energy! I need to get out of this body, because it is very tired. I don't think I had a single free day. It was such hard labor, with less and less personal stimuli, because my work took over. I went on like a machine during the last years.*

L: What happens with you now?

R: *Strange, I do not feel scared, just numb. I think I go in and out of my body. I go out and I travel. I experience things and then I return. Time does not matter at all. I am half dead in a way. Yes, the body gives up easily. There is nobody around, except the nurses. I sneak out in the middle of the night. Nobody there. I think I have been half-out, half-in, for a long time.*

L: Helen, can you help me understand now if you have some similarities with your present incarnation as Rita?

R: *I feel proud in one way, but on the other hand, I did not take care of myself. This tendency to be a workaholic is in Rita's life, too. As Helen, I do not live my own life, but I give up myself completely. Completely! It is only the moments with Fritz, the few moments, when I can relax a little.*

But then I went home to my place, and he went home to his family. He had a family. In that way, it was more ... even though I am a woman ... I am more like a man in that sense ... because I did no feminine things – whatever that would be, but anyway, I did not care to dress nicely and I used to work in my work outfit all the time. How boring is that?

L: What makes you finally die?

R: *I sneak out in the middle of the night! For a moment, I look from above at the hospital where I worked all my life. It is wonderful to move around so freely. Not to be in that skinny body anymore. The nurses have not noticed yet that I am dead. I just move about for a while to say goodbye and then I am ready to move on in the morning. I was a workaholic, so I have some problems leaving the hospital, even though I have died. What worries me is that there is nobody who can carry on my work when I die.*

L: Sorry to hear that you are worried. Is there anything that could make your departure easier?

R: *Strange, but it feels like I did not really teach anybody. It is like a secret. It is strange. Yes, I don't have time to stay here any longer! I must move on now! There were a few nurses that understood. They are sad when they find me dead. Yes, they will remember. And they are thinking of me. I now see a movie about the life in the hospital and with those who were kind of enemies. They were happy when I died – but it doesn't matter anymore now. I only feel a relief to leave all this behind. I have started to distance myself more and more from it. Now I am in a hurry again.* (Laughs.) *It actually was hard to leave the hospital but I finally let go.*

Restoration and reflection

Numbers of you are looking for
a state of "peace" in which there is
a static sort of bliss, with all questions forever
answered and all problems solved.
Some of you think that this will somehow
be miraculously accomplished for you.
If you recognized the power of your own being,
you would know that it ever seeks greater realms
of creativity and experience, in which
new challenges are inherent – for all problems
are challenges.

JANE ROBERTS: *THE NATURE OF PERSONAL REALITY*

Most of my clients go to a "place of restoration" after a life lived. In my life as Helen, my body was very worn out. Just like stepping out of a costume that would have been perfect for a role in a screenplay. It felt great to leave the skinny and worn out body of Helen behind and be free again.

Helen died in the hospital where she had worked all her life. After her death, it was difficult for her, as a soul, to leave her body behind. She wanted to linger and make sure that her patients in the hospital were taken care of. It was very nice to feel the support from my LBL facilitator during the phase when I, as Helen, had doubts to leave the hospital after I died.

This is what I report to my LBL facilitator after my passing as the hard-working doctor Helen and finally travel to Soul Home willingly.

LBL facilitator: Helen, please tell me how you feel after you have left your body behind in the hospital bed!

Rita: *I have a feeling of being carried away so nicely. The one that holds me has a very light and sensitive touch simultaneously, and it feels safe. A light touch! It is a specialist in holding. I have a feeling that I have been taken to a place of rest. It is not like a hospital, but it is a place for ... The one that was carrying me leaves.*

L: How did it feel to be carried like that?

R: *Those who are here specialize in taking care of those who are tired, those who have been in war and those who have worked too hard. It is a place where exhausted souls can rest. It feels like I am floating around, but also that I have my place. It is not like a bed, more like a place where you would dock, as* *one imagines you would in a spaceship. This is my dock and this is where I recharge.*

L: Sounds wonderful that you are taken so well care of now!

R: *Yes, it takes a while, because for a long time I used all my reserves working, so I need help to get extra energy. I am very worn out.*

L: Can you explain what Helen and your present incarnation Rita have in common?

R: *Rita has learnt to raise her energy a little with meditation and other methods, while for Helen, dealing with childbirths was like a drug. She was rejuvenated by each childbirth that went well. It is the same for Rita. Rita raises her energy when she knows a client is on the way to her. "Must prepare!" And, in a way, it spills over on herself.*

Burnout syndrome as a learning experience

How well I know with what burning intensity you live. You have experienced many lives already, including several you have shared with me – full rich lives from birth to death, and you just have to have these rest periods in between.

Anaïs Nin

I was surprised how much I recognized the behavior of Helen in my life as Rita. Since childhood, I had that passion to work with something that gives me a deeper meaning. When I believe in something I devote myself completely. Sometimes too much! The question after my experience as Helen was if I had learned anything from my several burnout experiences? Did I work hard to avoid my deep feeling of sadness and loneliness or was the strong urge to "save the world" a way to escape from my own perhaps boring and lonely reality? I was not sure what my "blind spots" were hiding from me.

I have concluded that my burnout did not mainly have physical causes. For me the reason to my burnout was WHY I worked so hard without rest. I learned that producing things and go for a goal is like breathing out. Giving myself enough sleep, loving relationships, enough of rest and fun is like breathing in. NO WONDER I got exhausted if I just kept breathing out and very seldom in. I had forgotten that I must recharge my batteries!

I believe LBL is one way for certain souls to discover and maybe find the underlying cause for their tendency to burn out. To connect with the soul again and balance the breathing can help. My two LBL sessions helped me recover from burn-out on a very deep level. After my LBL sessions my intuition became stronger and I received profound contact with my inner guidance. The phenomenon of grace came into my life and I learned how to ask for guidance and to embrace the help I received. With the help of LBL I learned that I need to take care of and listen to the voice of my inner child.

In popular psychology and analytical psychology, "inner child" is our childlike aspect. It includes all that we learned and experienced as children, before puberty. The inner child denotes a semi-independent entity subordinate to the waking conscious mind.

An LBL case story

The Surgeon

Imagine there's no heaven
It's easy if you try
No hell below us
Above us only sky
Imagine all the people living for today
Imagine there's no countries
It isn't hard to do
Nothing to kill or die for
And no religion too
Imagine all the people living life in peace
You may say I'm a dreamer
But I'm not the only one
I hope someday you'll join us
And the world will be as one

John Lennon

The fortyfive-year-old surgeon scheduled an LBL with me after he had read the books of Dr. Newton. A husband and father, with a promising career in the fields of surgery and medical research, what he lacks most is time. A spiritual calling and a strong urge to be of service for a "higher good" were included in his list of what to explore in his first LBL.

"I am open to what may come of the session", he said. An open mind is always a good start, I thought.

Here is a dialogue from a passage in his first LBL. The Surgeon is in a past life as a soldier, a "killing machine", named Ray.

Rita: Why did you incarnate as a soldier, Ray?

Surgeon: *I had a mission. I was one of the thousands of souls that had to descend at the time. We had to take a stand against this. There was a choice from the beginning. We knew this would come and I had to be part of it. Not because evil wins, but because the power of evil was very strong. It was a choice. For me this goes without saying. I did not have anything to learn from the battlefield, but I did what I had to do.*

R: So Ray, what you are saying is that many souls descended at this moment in time. May I ask if you are aware right now of what the underlying reason is that so many souls descend to earth and take part in a certain historical event as a war for example?

S: *It is all about education! It is like a school!* (Laughs out loud.) *It is terrible but ... imagine that you act out to be a teacher, but you do not, or maybe you do, but if you descend with experience you are not affected so badly by it. You just go in there. The others, they suffer, they are tormented and experience all the bad things ... you are also a part in it, but it does not "get to you". But it "gets to" the other people, they learn from it, sadly they must experience this suffering, so that enough people will realize that we do not want this anymore.*

R: So when you descend as Ray you have a specific mission and you are not affected like those who learn something from the suffering they go through. Did I get this right?

S: *Yes, that's right. In this specific case, I did not descend to learn something. I descended because "force must descend". That is the way I'd like to express myself about this.*

R: Okay, so force must descend? Can you explain what this means?

S: *It is not just me, but many, many others who choose this way.*

R: I am curious to know if anybody organizes this in the spirit world – that so many shall descend when a thing like this is about to happen. Or does every individual soul feel a calling, or something like that?

S: *The information I get is that we feel what is happening on earth when we are in afterlife. We do see and know, you see, because here we are not disconnected. This depends on our level; how much we are part of what happens on earth. Well I am not, but there are those who are taking part in it, they try to push things into the right direction. We are able to choose very destructive ways and this was a very destructive one (meaning WW2) and huge sacrifices were demanded from many.*

Childhood memories

We enter the world as vulnerable infants – helpless and utterly dependent on adults for getting all our needs met. We need to be nurtured, protected, and loved – emotionally and physically. And even though we grow in size, that sensitive and fragile little beeing never disappears. Usually hidden, it lives on and waits for us to reclaim it.

Lucia Capacchione Ph.D.: *Recovery of your inner child*

The initial phase of the LBL includes the "warming up" of soul memories. In hypnosis, there is no sense of time, so for most of my clients it is a quite natural process to regress to childhood. The Surgeon is now back perceiving himself as a twelve-year-old boy.

Rita: You are now twelve years old! Please tell me where are you now!

Surgeon: *I like to sit by my desk when I look out of the window. I am not sure if it is only a meadow ... or if it is ... well, this is where I like to sit.*

R: Tell me how you feel!

S: *When I sit in bed I feel sad.*

R: You feel sad? Please tell me more about yourself! Do you have any friends?

S: *I have a lot of friends, but deep inside I feel very lonely. Nevertheless, I like activities and it's never hard for me to find friends. That is the kind of boy I am now. I have good friends here, where we live. But I feel ... insecure. Well, why is that?*

R: Yes, why is that?

S: *I feel very, very lonely. There are no negative incidents. It is just a feeling, sitting on my bed. A feeling! It sounds strange, but I feel very lonely.*

R: Can you tell me how come you feel like this?

S: *I genuinely miss a fixed point – I mean a person. It is like there is no one for me ... I cannot reach anybody.*

R: Is is difficult for you now?

S: *It is some kind of combination. I do not see anybody that I can get close to, and nobody get closer to me.*

R: Do you know if you miss anything?

S: *What I miss is joy and laughter.*

R: Can you help me understand a little more about the way you are right now?

S: *I am a person who is quite serious. I am not the one who creates this joy. I need a compensation. I need someone who can help me fill this gap a little. And there is nobody nearby, although I do receive a little bit of it from grandma and grandpa. Especially grandma has it in her.*

R: This sounds nice ...

S: *Yes. Where I am ... I am rather burdened. I think. Not in a negative way – but burdened, responsible, serious, deep. I need balance from outside and this I cannot manage by myself.*

R: Please tell me something more about yourself!

S: *I see a picture of the time I sprained my foot when I was nine or ten years old. My feeling is that I am with grandpa and grandma and I can rest when I am with them. I can rest and I feel safe. I can just BE there. Strange! But I can be who I am. That is the best way I can explain it: that I can "just be". It is not based on deep discussions or anything like that, but I am just there and rest there. This is how I can express it: I rest when I am with them.*

It is war

We continue to an even younger age. Here is a dialogue with the Surgeon when he is a seven-year-old boy.

Rita: Would you like to tell me what you enjoy doing now when you are seven?

Surgeon: *It has very much to do with war. Indians and things like that. Cowboys! And a lot of soldiers!*

R: Sounds like fun! Can you tell me more?

S: *We play with small figures and we run around outside in the woods as well. Mostly it is Indians and cowboys, maybe a rifle, maybe a hat. Sometimes we have shotguns ...*

R: That is nice! Continue please!

S: *I get so many pictures now. I am mostly busy with arranging small figures to play with. I enjoy it very much. Now I am aware of building things with my small soldiers and arranging them as I would like them. Now I feel I am in this picture.*

R: Very good! Tell me what happens!

S: *They look like small, small soldiers. They look like they are from ... the second world war.*

R: Aha! Continue please!

S: *It is not like a routine, but ... what can I say ... I tend to arrange them the same way every time. I do not understand why I like to play this way and I ask myself this question now and the answer is: "therapy". Now words keep coming inside me and I hear the word: "need ". This is kind of good for me.*

R: Tell me more!

S: *There are so many soldiers that I play with. Often, often, often. I do not always arrange them the same way, but in a very similar way.*

R: How do you arrange them generally?

S: *I am always one of the allies. Yes, we are the good ones, always fighting against the Germans. Yes, always. There are the Japanese, too.*

R: Do you play this game alone or with others?

S: *This is my game. As a matter of fact, it is a game I play alone. Yes! I always start with putting all the men into proper positions. Then I must make sure that the good guys win every time. And so, they seem to, every single time.*

R: Do you make any sounds when you play?

S: *"'Ra-ta-ta-ta-ta". And "boom" and sounds like that! I think there is very much machine gun there.*

R: How do you feel when you make the sounds?

S: *The feeling is that this comes very naturally. It's like a habit. It's not pleasant – but natural and obvious. These are the words I get now. It is about needs.*

R: So this is what you do very often? Is this something that feels familiar to you?

S: *Yes. When the game is over it seems that there are many dead* (laughs). *Ha ... but they are just made of plastic!* (Sounds relieved.)

R: How do you know when the game is over?

S: *It is when most of the Germans are dead, you know.*

R: Okay, thank you for letting me know this. Is there anything else that you would like to investigate now, when you are seven?

S: *No, things are alright. I feel actually quite alright and relaxed after all.*

Telling me about his games with plastic soldiers, the Surgeon has already been in deep hypnosis for about one and a half hour. I notice that he seems to relax nicely as we go along. So, I decide to regress him deeper into a younger age.

I can crawl-stand-sit!

I invite the Surgeon to go back to the time when he is one or two years of age. Here is what he is telling me:

Rita: Please tell me about your first happy memory as a baby!

Surgeon: *The feeling is that I am crawling and looking up at my mother, who laughs. Happy! She seems genuinely happy about the fact that I appear around the corner.*

R: Tell me, can you stand on your feet now?

S: *I crawl-stand-sit. I cannot really say. I think I can stand. I don't know if I can walk, but I can crawl.*

R: What is your mummy like?

S: *Yes, mummy is genuinely, genuinely happy that I exist.*

R: Sounds lovely!

S: *What can I say? I feel happy that I can make her happy. This is how it feels.*

There is very little space in here!

Dr. Newton created the LBL method, which includes regressing to childhood and then to the time as a fetus just before birth. He found that this procedure makes it easier for the human mind to relax. The mind cannot grasp how it can be possible to remember a time as early in life as being an unborn child, but for the soul this is not a problem.

This is what the Surgeon reports from inside his mother's womb:

Rita: What does is feel like right now?

Surgeon: *Yes. It feels alright, but there is very little space in here ... Yes, but still I have a feeling of freedom. Strange ... I do not feel stuck; not completely. I do not feel locked up.*

R: Okey, very good. Please tell me more about what you perceive!

S: *I do not feel as if I am in the birth canal. The time has not come yet, I can still move freely. I can move. I am not in fixed position.*

R: You said before that it is not a good idea to enter the new body too early with your soul. Where were you before you entered your new body as the Surgeon?

Here my client all of a sudden starts to talk about a state similar to death, but from the perspective of birth as the Surgeon.

S: *I have a feeling that I rest. But it is just a feeling. I see a picture of a bed. There are ... individuals standing around me and it feels like I am lying down and about to die, even if I am not. It is not a negative thing. It is almost like you would see an old person who is about to die – to give you a picture of the kind of rest, I mean.*

R: Thank you for telling me all this. What more do you know? Tell me more!

S: *There are many people, not a lot – maybe 10-15 – around my bed. They support me. Can this be right that I am about to descend?*

R: Yes, do you know if this seems right?

S: *The answer is that I am in the spirit world now and about to incarnate. Because I clearly feel that this is not an earth-bound experience. I cannot tell you anymore. But I don't feel this is earth and that I am about to leave earth. There are people I recognize now!*

R: Tell me who they are!

S: (Sighs.) *I cannot see.*

R: Please go deeper and then tell me!

S: *Somewhere I see F (the wife of S) here.*

All of a sudden a lot of emotions come through:

S: (Groans and says with a high-pitched voice, cries, then says:) *I am sad, because I don't want to incarnate.* (Sighs, cries.)

R: Why are you so reluctant to incarnate?

S: (Says with a high-pitched voice:) *The plan is to grow and open up myself, I think. But I am tired!! I am tired of incarnation!*

R: Have you reincarnated many times?

S: *Oh yes! I think so! That is how it feels!*

R: So you'd rather not?

S: *I have a feeling now – when I see myself in the bed just like an old person – that I am done with this: I am finished. I have the same feeling now, but I am going the other way. It is not only a negative thing. There is a lot of positive energy in it.*

R: What happens now?

S: *Oh, damn it all, I say!* (Cries loudly.)

I really do not want to go down to earth!
OOOOh damn it! I hate that place!

R: You can just relax now. (I deepen his hypnotic state and there is a long silence when he seems to rest.) Please try to give me the information as to whether you have incarnated many times before!

S: *Yes! But there are other places. There are other places, but I cannot tell you if I go there or not. You can do other things, but for some reason I must do just this, but I cannot tell you why. But there is so much pain. There is so much pain and I don't know if I ... it is almost unbearable.*

R: Could we check if there is anybody around your bed that supports you when you feel this way?

S: *Yes, F is one of them* (the wife of S). *They are all here around the bed to help me. Well, we have decided to meet. This is how it is!*

R: So have you already decided here in your bed that you will meet later with some of them during your life as S?

S: *The answer is: "Later!" I have to experience a lot first. I have to descend into the mud. I must get burned a little, to burn away the harshness. No, it is the environment that is harsh. But I must open. I must open more. It is a hard nut to crack.*

R: You told me about the feeling you have now – lying in a bed like an old person ready to die, but you are going the other way to be born. Did I get this right?

S: *Yes. Now I am back in the womb of my mother. I go in and out. It feels like I am in here tasting it a little and then ...sometimes I return to the "Rest place". Because I don't want to ...*

R: What is the most important thing to understand for S with all that you are telling me now?

S: *"Trust", is the word I get.*

R: Is there something else about this new body of S that you would like to tell me?

S: *It is actually quite sensitive. It must be looked after ... it must move, otherwise it stiffens and becomes ... This body really must move or it will not work well. It has to do with the raw material. The heritage! The raw material is fairly good in my case, but it has to be looked after. Certain materials you can neglect, but they still last quite well, but this raw material you have to take care of or otherwise it will not last.*

R: Yes S, that is interesting to hear! Please tell me more!

S: *You might get a body that can endure a lot. This one endures quite a lot of thrashing, but you can get a body that en-*

dures thrashing or be neglected. It does not have to be cleaned and polished, but it lasts anyway. However, this body should be cleaned, polished and maintained. If it is done, it works better. Do you understand what I am saying?

R: I think I do! What else do you want to tell me now?

S: *"Humility!" If I had a perfect body, there would be a risk that my ego would become too large. If the body did not have any limitations and I had been able to put much more into action, then the risk would be great that my ego would have been greatly inflated, too early. And in that case, I might have lost my way!*

It is quite common that I hear the client talking about the present incarnation from another awareness that seems wiser. They are talking about themselves as third person which is fascinating to hear. When I ask them, who is the identity that reports to me, they often answer that it is their soul-self. Of course, as a doctor, the Surgeon knows how to take care of his physical body, but still in his hypnotic state he reminds himself of the facts and the risk of over-inflating his ego. He also talks about timing. This is an example of how it is possible to have a dual awareness in hypnosis. It is often very interesting to perceive oneself as a child, a fetus or as a past life personality and still comment on it as an adult or in this case as a professional surgeon.

We cannot put up with this

*I know not with what weapons World War III will
be fought, but World War IV will be fought with
sticks and stones.*

Albert Einstein

Now we proceed to follow the Surgeon to his most recent past life (from what he reported under hypnosis) as the soldier Ray in WW2.

Rita: Please tell me the first thing you are aware of now?

Surgeon: *A weapon! I am holding a machine gun. It is a fairly modern weapon.*

R: Can you make the sound, so I can hear what the weapon sounds like, when you use it?

S: *Ra-ta-ta-ta- ta* (sounds the same as he did with his mouth as a seven-year-old).

R: So what else are you aware of?

S: *It feels like I am in a desert. I wear shirt or jacket, but* *nothing on my forearms. I wear some kind of ... when I look down I see shorts. Or I don't know ... but I don't wear trousers. I have some kind of boots. Some kind of shorts. Not any giant high boots, but they look almost like leggings. I feel very experienced in this! I know how to do it. Yuk!*

R: What kind of body sensations do you have?

S: *My body is well-functioning. It is. There are those that are better. But this is not a decrepit body. It is a strong body. It is at 4,5 on a 5 scale. It is strong and well trained, a mortal body. It knows how to kill. It has done it all!*

R: Are you some kind of professional soldier?

S: *No. It feels like WW2, but it is just a feeling.*

R: How old are you now?

S: *Not yet thirty, just before. I feel very experienced though.*

R: Do you have a feeling that you enjoy this?

S: *No, I don't like it. I just do it.*

R: Is it out of duty?

S: *No, that word is not right ... there is no choice; I cannot choose anything else. This is how it is. No duty, I just must do it. This evil just must be removed. It is a simple fact. If it is a duty,* *it is almost stronger than duty. A duty you can run away from, but this feels like an obligation to attend to, clean out and finish. We cannot put up with this!!*

R: Which elements have to be cleaned out?

S: *It is Hitler, it feels. It feels like I am British.*

R: So right now you are in a desert?

S: *Yes!*

R: Would you please tell me what is going on around you now?

S: *In this moment I see nothing. I just feel that the killing has been going on forever. It feels like I have been killing and have killed and killed. I do not suffer. I just do it. I feel rather empty in this. That is the way it feels. I am good at it!*

R: Okay, thank you for letting me know how you feel! Would you like to tell me your name?

S: *Ray!*

R: And your surname?

S: *Maybe Lesley.*

R: May I call you Ray now?

S: *That's okay with me!*

R: Please tell me what you are aware of right now on a deeper level, Ray?

S: *It feels like I knew this before I incarnated. I feel I know this would be a huge part of my life as Ray. And it feels like I did not want to do it, but that I choose it because I knew that many people had to choose this way.*

R: You seem to have a strong conviction in what you call "the evil has to be removed". Have I got this right, Ray?

S: *Well it is not "they", but more the evil as such. It is not about them, because they are not evil. It is just that this way to do it, does not work. We cannot have it this way. I do not want to do this, but we must clean this out. Well, I guess I'll take it then! Someone, somehow, and I wish I could avoid it. I don't want to! I know that I have the skills and I know that I am TERRIBLY good at it. Yuk!*

R: Can you tell me if you see any similarities between your personality as a surgeon (S) today and your personality as Ray?

S: *Yes, it is what we call a sense of duty that we share. But it is also this talent to ... focus. Somehow my contact with this life as Ray makes ... it is a feeling that I have it in my hands ... I mean as S.*

R: May I ask and share this reflection when S works as a surgeon holding a knife, there is perhaps a similar precision as when Ray holds a machine gun?

S: *The focus when the situation is serious is the same. No matter what I do, it is about staying cool, if I may say so. To stay present and to be very focused. This also has to do with survival – of oneself or the one you are dealing with. It is a very positive thing.*

R: And Ray, you seem to be convinced what you do here is necessary, because evil has to be removed. It is "all or nothing", so to speak.

S: *No, not "all or nothing", but for a long time it is what it seems to be. And things do not last forever. But there must be an end to this, so I give all I have. Yes, in a way it is all or nothing. Things can go down the drain, really.*

R: Now Ray, is there anything important in particular that you would like to focus on?

S: *I see that I am the reason why many people get killed. I am partly dissociated, but I am not one of those who kill because they like doing it. I do not want to do more than I should, but what I do is terrible. I do ... it is not that evil killing ... this sounds strange when I say it but, there are those who like to do it and* *go on with it and do more than necessary. I still feel that I have an inner conviction in what I do.*

R: Well Ray, you feel you have performed your mission, so to speak. Is that how it is?

S: *Yes, well that is a way of putting it. I absolutely do not want to torment those whom we captured. Not more than we absolutely must. I think it has to do with trying to be honest…*

R: Please tell me what rank you have as a soldier here!

S: *A sergeant or a captain. I am not a common soldier. It feels like I am a captain. And I have a couple of boys that I oversee. But I feel a sense of equality with them.*

R: Are there any souls you recognize in your men? Maybe someone who is also known in your life as S, Roy?

S: *It is Ray!*

R: Sorry for my mistake, Ray!

Author's note: The Surgeon gets angry with me for my mistake of calling him Roy instead of Ray. He seems to identify totally with his past life personality and is very picky with me making this mistake. This felt very different from the personality of the Surgeon.

S: *Yes, I think I met M in my S life! I see him now. He was a classmate in medical school, like a brother.*

R: Is he also in the military, Ray?

S: *It feels like we are equals, I am not sure if he is below or above me in rank. But we are very close and popular, too. It seems that we are a special group; we are not one ordinary group, more like elite soldiers.*

R: What is your mission in the desert?

S: *It is about going behind enemy lines. We do small raids and scout.*

R: Can you tell me in which country you are now?

S: *We are in Egypt, Libya ...*

R: What name do you call M, who is the medical friend in your S life, Ray?

S: *Tom!*

R: What does Tom look like?

S: *He is a bit skinnier than me.*

R: Do you save each other's lives sometimes, you and Tom?

S: *Without seeing when, I have a feeling we have done that a lot of times.*

R: So you trust each other?

S: *Yes, a 100 percent. Somewhere I see H, too. He is also an old friend of S.*

R: I can understand that the situation you are in now Ray, is all about knowing whom you can trust.

S: *But M, he is like another part of me, really.*

R: Is F (the wife of S) in Ray's life?

S: *No.*

R: Is there a woman in your life, Ray?

S: *No.*

R: Is it okay now to move forward in time to the last day in your life, Ray? How old are you when you die?

S: *I don't grow old!*

R: How old are you now on the day of your death?

S: *Thirty maybe.*

The following in the dialogue, I already shared in part 2.

Rita: So, what happens now?

Surgeon: *I have a lot of bullets in my abdomen.*

R: Do you die right away from this?

S: *No. It feels like the whole right part of me is wounded.*

R: Can you feel it now? What has happened?

S: (Sighs.) *Let me look! It feels as my right leg below the knee is hanging like a rag doll. It looks as it exploded in some way, now totally shattered. I have bullets in my abdomen and it feels like I have bullets that also have penetrated right through my back. Then there is something wrong with my right hand, but I cannot see that now. I will not live much longer.*

I am neither sad nor … I am in quite a lot of pain, I feel.

R: What is it that finally causes your death?

S: *I am bleeding somewhere in the abdomen, but I do not bleed a lot. That is strange. It feels like I manage for a couple of hours. But I am lying alone somehow.*

R: Ray, can you please use your knowledge as a surgeon and give me a diagnosis of the medical state of Ray?

S: *When I look at myself from the outside, I notice many bullet wounds in the abdomen that have broken the blood vessels, there are intestines that are wounded and I also have my legs all shattered by bullets, well partly, but those blood vessels are in cramp – they do not bleed anymore, so I won't bleed to death. In the same way, I have a few injuries in my arms, the right one ... that ... and why it is only the right side I do not know. All this is not going to make me die right away, but I will die soon, within a day at most.*

R: Is it day or night time?

S: *It feels like it is at night and I am lying here looking and I know that I am going to die. I cannot end it, but will just have to wait. I am not afraid!*

R: Very good Ray, thank you for reporting all this to me now!

S: *It feels good!*

R: Well that is nice! Would it be possible now to let go of your shattered body and die, Ray?

S: *Yes!*

Death scene

*I'm not afraid of death; I just don't want to be there
when it happens.*

Woody Allen

It might seem strange, but in an LBL session it is possible to experience what it is like to die, and at the same time to report to me about it as it happens. This is only possible if we go through the death of a past life, because obviously, it is not possible to go there from a life we still live in. That would confuse the mind. Dr. Newton called this technique "to enter into soul home from the front door".

At this phase of an LBL, we go to the death scene of the past life. In the case of Ray, his body is mortally wounded and the only way to move forward logically is to leave the body behind. In many other cases, my clients go to past lives where they lived quite ordinarily and die peacefully in old age, surrounded by family and loved ones. But in this case death is caused by violence in war.

Rita: Have you left the earth plane now?

Surgeon: *Yes, I have left it already a while ago* (in real time only a few seconds has passed from his report of the injuries). *The feeling is that I am travelling in some kind of tunnel. I do not have a defined sense of myself. It is like I am just a point. It feels as if I am past my body now.*

R: Tell me how you move!

S: *It feels like I just want to move forward now and have passed a few stations during our conversation ... it also feels like I am getting closer to something or have landed on something. Landed, is the word I can use.*

Death

I have tried to show death from the perspective of the soul to ease the pain of those left behind. As Plato said, "Once free of the body, the soul is able to see truth clearly because it is purer than before and recalls the pure ideas which it knew before." Survivors must learn to function again without the physical presence of the person they loved by trusting the departed soul is still with them. Acceptance of loss comes one day at a time. Healing is a progression of mental steps that begins with having faith that you are not truly alone. To complete the life contract, you made in advance with the departed, it is necessary to rejoin the rest of humanity as an active participant. You will see your love again soon enough. I am hopeful my years of research into the life we live as souls may assist survivors in recognizing that death only exchanges one reality for another in the long continuum of existence.

MICHAEL NEWTON: *DESTINY OF SOULS: NEW CASE STUDIES OF LIFE BETWEEN LIVES*

When I was young I was very scared of death. The fact that I one day would not be around anymore was unbearable. As a young nurse, I was naturally confronted with death among my patients, but I was thinking that death had nothing to do with me.

When I was about forty, I decided to work at Maria Regina, a hospice for the terminally ill, just outside Stockholm. Although I had many obligations as a nurse with all sorts of medical duties, I also had the privilege to sit at the bedsides of dying patients. I learned what it felt like to talk with someone who had accepted their own death, and with some who had not. I remember that I often thought it might be a good idea to try to be a friend of death while still being healthy and young. When I witnessed death happening, it was obvious that after the last breath the body looked and felt like an empty shell. I felt the same when my father died in 1986.

An LBL is a way to make your acquaintance with death. After the LBL you have still the rest of your life to live – maybe with a little less fear of death. One could say that it is a way to "peek" into the afterlife without dying. It is like an organized Near Death Experience.

When I was working at Maria Regina, I often thought I would like to have that inner peace which I felt in patients, who had accepted their death and destiny when their time had come.

Goodbye to loved ones

*The ideal death, I think, is what was the ideal
Victorian death, you know, with your grandchildren
around you, a bit of sobbing. And you say goodbye
to your loved ones, making certain that one of them
has been left behind to look after the shop.*

TERRY PRATCHETT

When the client has crossed over in the death moment, I ask
if they have some unfinished business or want to say goodbye
to anybody before continuing their journey to the afterlife.
Here is a conversation with the Surgeon in this phase of his
LBL.

Rita: Ray, is there someone down there on earth you would
like to say goodbye to now that you died?

Surgeon: *My friend V is there somewhere.*

R: Do you feel any need now to say goodbye to him?

S: *No. He also suffers. He is in a similar situation to Ray.*

R: Who was V in your life, Ray?

S: *He is somewhere there in my surroundings, but I cannot see now, really. But it feels as though he also dies there and then, maybe not. But he is not getting old – though nobody else is either. It is only him. It feels like we all moved on from there.*

It was just everyone! Not only there and then, but ... there was no use to linger there any longer.

Entrance to Spirit world and beyond

Dr. Michael Newton discovered, mapped and structured the journey of souls in the afterlife. One of his great findings was a consistency in what his 7,000 clients told him about their journey after death. During my years as an LBL facilitator, I have heard many clients prove this consistency to be true.

We will now continue to follow Ray after his death on the battlefield and ascension from his body and entry into the afterlife.

Rita: Can you tell me what you experience now, Ray?

Surgeon: *I cannot say exactly what I experience. It feels like there is a very bright light. Yes. It is such a bright light ... a force that receives me. The picture I see now is like in "The Fellowship of the Ring" ... it reminds me of the woman there who is an elf. This feeling is similar, but it is not her that I see.*

R: Sounds wonderful! Go on ...

S: *A feminine force it surely is ... a princess that has come to greet and welcome me back. The feeling is like a garden, but it is not a garden, because there are no trees in a way, but still there are trees. But I am not sad. I am just happy.*

R: Is the feminine force familiar to you?

S: *There is a sense of recognition. I see a picture of a hand. The hand is on my cheek and this is symbolic. But it is not the feeling of a mother taking care of her son, but more like ... not lovers, but as very, very dear friends, who meet.*

R: Does she have any particular colours?

S: *The whole thing is purple – blue somehow.*

R: Would you like to tell me the name of your dear old, sweet elflike friend?

S: *Her name is Avron. She just said "thank you" in a strong voice.*

R: Why do you think that she is thanking you?

S: *Because I took on this thing and went down. Because the feeling is that I did not only have to learn a lot. I also knew I would descend to do this because I know it so well. I know how to be a soldier. I can kill!*

R: You can kill and now as Surgeon you know how to save lives. Right?

S: *This one can turn around and maybe I did, but the feeling she conveys was to thank me because I descended and did my job!* (Laughs out loud.) *I am just happy to be back!*

Names of souls and Guides

In a lot of cases the clients meet their Guide at the stage of their LBL journey when they have crossed over. In certain other cases, the Guide shows up later along the way. The Surgeon meets his beautiful soul friend Avron and not his Guide, after his death as Ray. He is quite surprised when he tells me that his soul name is Vairy and the name of his soul friend is Avron.

Rita: Do you recognize the elflike figure you just met?

Surgeon: *It feels like we are the same.*

R:　Is she some kind of soulmate?

S:　*No. Actually she is a little more advanced than me.*

R:　What is she like? Do you recognize her?

S:　*Could it be K?*

R:　Who is that?

S:　*Yes, I do not know.*

R:　Is it someone that S knows?

S: *Yes!* (Seems deeply focused.) *It is an old friend that I have always felt very close to. But I do not know. I do not dare to answer!*

R: Would you like to describe her so I can understand what she looks like?

S: *She is soft and very feminine. And so wise! It is like talking to someone you can discuss anything with. We know each other so well. So well!*

R: What does she call you where you are now? What is your soul name?

S: *Vairy. How strange!*

R: Well, you can talk about anything, you said. What will you talk about with Avron now, Vairy?

S: *We talk a lot about the meaning of descending or not to a life on earth.*

R: Do you know if Avron still incarnates or if she does not?

S: *It feels as if she does, occasionally.*

A healing shower

When a soul once again returns to a pure energy state in the spirit world, it no longer feels hate, anger, envy, jealousy and the like. It has come to Earth to experience these sorts of emotions and learn from them.

Michael Newton, Ph.D.

When the client enters the Spirit world after the gate of death and meets his Guide or another entity in a soul state, they are often first taken to a place of restoration.

Especially after the death of a hard life the extra need for recovery and restoration for the soul seems necessary. Dr. Newton writes that in many cases there is an experience of having a healing shower. The recovery after a past life death is in most cases also a very healing experience for the present body of the client lying on my couch. From what the clients tell me, the restoration of energy after a life lived is very pleasant.

My own experience from my first LBL in this phase of my soul journey, was that I saw a small building that looked like a holy Asian pagoda (small temple). I just knew that in there my total soul energy was kept and stored. My Guide who met me when I returned to the spirit world, invited me to step into the pagoda to revitalize. I did not hesitate to enter. Once inside the pagoda, it was like standing in a pillar of white light. A strong feeling of cleansing, healing, recovery and restoration came over me, all at the same time.

Some clients tell me that their soul group meets them when they return. There is often a feeling of celebration and joy after a life lived. I often hear them tell me about the unconditional acceptance and love that radiates from their loved ones, who welcome them back home after a life.

The Surgeon says that he does not have a strong need for recovery and restoration after his short life as Ray. Dr. Newton describes that some souls decide to incarnate for a certain mission, rather than for personal development. Here is what the Surgeon says about this.

Rita: How do you feel? Are you tired?

Surgeon: *A little. Not very tired! It feels like I was restored as soon as I came back here, actually ... Then that symbolic tap on the cheek from Avron and I felt just well again.*

R: Can you tell me the reason why you seem to recover so fast?

S: *I am not bound to my body. Some souls are not. I am in a body occasionally and have just been with Ray for a while.*

R: Do I draw the right conclusion here, wondering if you have incarnated many times so you have practised often to die, so to speak?

S: *Far too many times. I do not want to be ... but I have done it a lot of times. Many, many times!* (Laughs out loud.) *I am just very happy to be back.*

Soul identity and
themes of the soul through times

Many years ago, I read an article about thirty Swedes who answered the following questions:

– Where would you like to live?

– With whom would you like to live?

– What would you like to work with?

I was surprised that none of them were happy with how they lived, worked or were doing at the time. If we choose and design our destiny before we incarnate, then why is it common that we often are so discontent with the result? To forget the "blueprint" seems to be part of the plan, so we can remember as we grow older and become wiser.

Michael Newton discovered that each soul has an identity, name and mission. We seem to become more and more specialized over time as we practise our skills again and again. When I first read Michael Newton's books, what interested me most was to find out if I have a general theme through my incarnations.

Here is a dialogue with the Surgeon concerning this matter:

Rita: I'd like to ask Avron this question about S! Why did S become a surgeon?

Surgeon: *It is because I was infinitely tired of all this killing. I had to do something else!*

R: You have told me that you played with little plastic soldiers very often as a child. Do you now know if there is anything you remember that made you play like this?

S: *I was reliving it! That is what it was all about. This is how I have felt as S about the life as Ray. I have felt that the Ray life has been very strong inside me, but not in a negative way. And I feel so done with it! Therefore, I chose something else within ... and now I have the privilege to have a medical profession. And I chose surgery because my body has the skill for it. Also, that it gives extra authority! But what do I need it for?*

R: Yes, what do you need it for? Yes, why particularly a surgeon?

S: *I see a diving board. A springboard. For me, or for something. I do not know for what. They tell me now that S is not there yet. He needs some more time! I hear: "He has to be older". Ah! Yes, they tell me it is not that far away. It has to do with experience. Not formal experience because this S already has, but a longer experience. I have to ascend to another step on earth.*

R: You have given us a very good insight into the life of Ray that you just lived and died in. Thank you!

S: *"You will understand!" "You don't have to know right now!" These are the words I hear. Well, what do I say about this?*

R: Yes, what do YOU say? Is this something YOU know now?

S: *Better not to know now! I am on the right track! "You are capable of more! And you will accomplish more!" This is what I know.*

R: May I ask whether the plan for S is somehow to prepare, or should he continue as before?

S: *The path is right, surgery is right, research is right but it feels heavy. Research will feel heavy, but it is right.*

R: Does research have to do with the kudos you were talking about before? What is the reason that S should continue with research if it feels heavy? Is S interested in it or does he do it as a part of his "mission"?

S: *He does it more like a mission. And interest. More the meaning, not for the ego, absolutely not. But I get the advice now to nourish my soul more!*

R: Let me take a moment to ask you who you are as a soul,

Vairy? Would you like to tell me about the characteristics of your soul?

S: *I have a hunger to learn new things. I also hear the words "old soul", if I may say so. I have been around for a long time. It feels like I am moving on from incarnating and I can almost say that I am done with it.*

R: Ah! You mean you are done with incarnation?

S: *Yes.*

R: Could you tell me what is left for S to accomplish in his present incarnation on earth?

S: *It feels like I have to take a stand for something. The words I get is that it is better not to know, because it can hurt. It could mean losses. The feeling is that you are not there yet, the time is not right. You will be there and you will understand.*

R: Is there a purpose with S being a surgeon when that day comes?

S: *Yes! So, to sum it up: Surgery and research nourish my soul! It is not necessary with more stillness. It is enough to go inwards. "You need your cave", we can put it this way: "You use too much energy to push yourself".*

R: Who says that you push yourself too much, Vairy?

S: *This is maybe what I am telling myself. I work too much and shall always do so. There is a risk that I can kill that drive.*

R: That is right! You are anxious to get a lot done!

S: *Yes! I hear: "Select your work. Focus on your work! Reduce your work and do it the right way!" My soul is not too severely crumbled. But there are a few dents if we should say something about it.*

R: Thank you Vairy, that sounds good. Maybe S knows how to rejuvenate in his daily life if he takes the chance to do so?

S: *Yes, he knows how to. He lies down and rests. He closes his eyes and listens to music. That is when he is recovering strength.*

R: I would like to know if you have a certain mission or theme that you are working with, Vairy. Do you have an out-sourcer that you work for?

S: *There is an old guy there somewhere. Avron and I are practically equals. It is like being 63 and 65 somehow. Well, she is a little bit ahead of me and she has a slightly different tone. But there are not oceans of wisdom between us. But there IS someone else, too.*

R: So what is your driving force when you incarnate into such a life? What is the core of the driving force?

S: *To teach others!*

R: Aha, okay.

S: *That is the reason why I am here as S, too. Among other reasons.*

I incarnate by free will, although in a way I really do not want to, because I am so tired of it that I ... Yes but I still do it for the sake of other people, but also for myself. Because I really think I am needed. Yes, that is a good way to put it. I know that I need to incarnate and I know that I have a task to fulfil.

Soul energy

Michael Newton discovered that we bring a certain percentage of our total soul energy with us into each incarnation and leave the rest behind in spirit world. When we return there we rejoin with the rest of our soul energy.

Michael Newton systematically asked his clients about the soul percentage they brought with them in the present incarnation and the past lives mentioned in their LBL. It seemed to vary between approximately 15-80 percent. If we would bring 100 percent into an incarnation, we would, according to Michael Newton, have no bridge to return after death. According to his research our "brain fuels" would burn with 100 percent soul energy taken into an incarnation.

One can say that while we are incarnated, we are simultaneously in our soul home because part of us are here on earth and part of us are still there. Could this be the reason why so many of my clients say that they feel they do not belong here? I hear this quite often. Maybe they long for the soul percentage left behind in spirit world?

Rita: How much soul energy did you bring into your S life, Vairy?

Surgeon: *It feels like I push a rather large percentage of my soul energy, but not all. I bring 2/3. I have to push rather much into it to be able to cope.*

R: How much did you bring into your Ray life?

S: *Spontaneously I would say it was not that much. Maybe 1/3.*

R: Why is that?

S: *That life was much clearer. I had only one task: to die in the battlefield. To do my very best in it. Not much more mental energy was needed. It was so clear. The darkness was so huge. The light had to take a stand and the decision was already made.*

Do we have favourite incarnations over time?

I personally like to ask my clients in an LBL if they had a favourite incarnation over time. The Surgeon told me about his favourite life as a famous poet and singer of divine songs. Remembering and reliving moments in a life that we lived to the fullest, might awaken memories that affect the present life. It is often said it is more difficult to be happy with what we have and to make use of our potential, than to spend a life complaining about circumstances and do nothing about it.

Rita: Would you like to tell me about the best body you ever had Vairy?

Surgeon: *It is a life where I was very talented in singing. I entertained. I had a beautiful voice.*

R: Did you express your soul through your voice?

S: *Yes.*

R: What period is it?

S: *I think somewhere between year 0 and before year 1000.*

R: What kind of songs do you sing?

S: *It feels like some kind of ... it is a very harmonious life. I sing and I write poetry. I feel appreciated, both for what I write and sing. Yes! It was a good life.*

R: Are you a woman or a man?

S: *I am a man! It feels like people experience my singing as a little divine. Like a joik* (a way of spiritual singing among the Sami people/Lapps in Scandinavia), *something like that ... this way of singing is timeless, actually.*

R: In your present life as a surgeon, you work with your hands. Here, your voice seems to be your tool. Your soul can express itself through poetry and song. Is it a clear voice? A high or a low-pitched voice?

S: *My voice is a deep tenor.*

R: Do you feel that you have a partner in this life as a singer?

S: *I have a family and children. I live a long life, a good life! I am very well known in this time and locality. I am popular and talked about over many years.*

R: Can you give examples of places where you perform?

S: *Both in temples and palacelike buildings ... larger buildings. It feels like it is Armenia or near there.*

R: Yes! So, you are a kind of "freelance temple singer" as we would say today? Not a monk nor a priest, but you let your voice be heard out of your own choice?

S: *I am very free and perform in many different places.*

R: That sounds fantastic! So if I get it right now your soul can communicate through beautiful divine singing! And you are well received! You communicate a divine feeling! Would you like to tell me how you could use this experience as a singer in your life as S?

S: *I dare to speak openly and to express myself freely. I want to be in contact with my voice thoroughly. This life reminds me of how to express myself and to stand up for what I express.*

PART 5

Integration

ALEKSANDR SOLZHENITSYN: *THE GULAG ARCHIPELAGO*

It was a pleasure to work with the Surgeon in a total of three LBL sessions in 2015 with a few months in between. He has been very helpful in commenting on his LBL experience. I would like to share his letters here as well as a dialogue in his second session.

A letter from the Surgeon
three months after his first LBL

Dear Rita,

I write to you after listening to the recording of my session several times, because I feel now that I am wide open to the misery of the world; unfortunately, it all goes right in, which has the effect on me that I feel increasingly heavy. One of the consequences of this is that I just want to escape into the inner world I found during the session, while knowing it is not the solution. In the same way, there is a longing for more hypnosis, I would say like a drug addict, who just wants more ...

One part of my "protection" is the garden and "the person" (Avron) I met there. When I return there, I find strength again.
My direction in life and the choices I made still stand solid, but the peace inside and the strength I felt after the session are totally gone, which is a strange feeling.

I am wondering if I need support in another hypnosis, or alternatively can I find inner stability by myself? What do you think Rita?

Warm regards
The Surgeon

During a phone call after I read his letter, we decided to schedule a second LBL. The purpose this time was to try to find out if there was a deeper explanation for his increased feeling of vulnerability.

The questions he brought to his first LBL were about finding out his direction in life and his priorities, because he was so busy with his responsibilities as a surgeon, medical researcher and father. At that time, his vulnerability was not an issue for him. Remembering a life as the soldier Ray, whose mission was to kill as many enemies as possible, seemed to have awakened something in him.

A passage from the second LBL
with the Surgeon

Here is a dialogue with the Surgeon back in afterlife speaking as his soul aspect Vairy:

Rita:	Would you like to tell me what you and Avron (elflike feminine soul friend from first LBL) do in the landscape where you are right now?

Surgeon: *We teach!*

R:	Aha! What do you teach?

S:	*It is almost like teaching them to read.*

R:	Would you like to tell me a little more about your teaching?

S:	*Yes, it is like a bunch of six-year-old kids playing football. They bounce around and do not know anything. Our job is to make them understand. I cannot explain this very well, but I have given you a picture.*

R:	So the feeling is that you teach six-year-old kids?

S: *Yes, almost like first to third grade. If you try to figure out what kind of souls we teach – I am giving you a symbolic meaning – a metaphor.*

R: Does this have to do with the phase of development they are in?

S: *Yes.*

R: Would you like to tell me if you and Avron are somehow specialized in your teaching? Do you only teach beginners, or do you also teach those who are more developed?

S: *We teach others, too. But it works in stages. It's like a school. Sometimes we meet those on the same level and then it's more of an exchange.*

R: Do you mean on the same level as you and Avron?

S: *Yes! Then the next stages are more like lectures and with these it is more advanced.*

R: Could you give me an example of a subject you teach beginners?

S: *Well, what I can tell you right away is that we teach them about the subject of ego (a person's sense of self-esteem or self-importance). The ego can make us stumble and take us away from the best of directions.*

R: Is it easier to stumble on ego issues if you are a beginner or if you are more advanced?

S: *You stumble constantly when you are a beginner. But the fall becomes so much bigger when you are more advanced, if I may say so. As an advanced soul, you incarnate with much more power. You can make things happen in a totally different way. Not always, but often this is the case. You can end up in a very bad situation if you go down with a lot of power and then the ego gets in the way.*

R: I understand! Can I ask you how the Surgeon relates to his ego?

S: *The feeling is that it does not disturb him. There was a risk earlier that the ego would have taken over, but in this phase of his life it is not a problem.*

R: Okay, thank you! When you and Avron teach, do you teach only in the spirit world or here on earth as well?

S: *This we do consciously and unconsciously in both places. But the teaching does not need to be in the same way here. The teaching can be by example, because you become a role model. It becomes more multifaceted in that way. You can do it in so many ways here.*

R: You have mentioned one way: as a role model. Can you tell me other ways of teaching?

S: *Yes, for example Mother Teresa is one type of a role model. She teaches by being. Now I only get these great ones, but Bill Gates has by his example shown us another way! If you look at the great ones, then there are lots of people who do a lot by their deeds. Even those who teach on all kinds of different levels – they actually mediate spiritual knowledge by their way of being.*

R: That's right. Nicely put! Is the teaching you and Avron create part of a bigger picture of cooperation with others who also teach something similar? Or is it just the two of you who do this?

S: *There are plenty who do this the same way we do. It feels almost like a conference, a huge plenary hall – conference is the right word, I think. There we meet like-minded souls and some-how mediate a kind of change of thoughts.*

R: Do those of you in the plenary hall have contact with each other as in a network? Do you know each other? Or could it be that everyone works individually?

S: *The purpose gives the answer. The purpose is that we must be independent and act independently. Sometimes the purpose is that we interact and become more powerful, if you would like to put it that way. It is also a combination. But we are not conscious of each other. Nevertheless, there is recognition if we meet! But even though you recognize someone it does not mean that you interact. You might even be antagonists!*

R: That's interesting! Thank you for explaining this so well. Please tell me if there is anything those in the plenary hall have in common?

S: *It is the level, in some way, the absolute beginners do not qualify to be here. They do not even get in. The key is to obtain a certain level and the only way to move forward is to understand.*

R: So what do they have to understand to qualify?

S: *Wow! Yes, I don't know, but the only thing is harmony. Harmony is the word.*

R: Is it possible that you and Avron can be in the plenary hall now?

S: *Yes, indeed. She is with me and I am there if I want to be.*

R: Is it possible to bring up questions for single members in there?

S: *Hmm ...*

R: Can I ask one of the Surgeon's questions?

S: *No, it would be the wrong forum. It is too large for small questions. There are smaller groups for that. This plenary hall is for the big events. It is for much bigger events.*

R: Can you go to a group that seems more relevant for asking the important questions for S?

S: *Yes, I can! Let me see. I cannot see it so clearly. Now we are there! It feels almost like I am upside down. I am there with Avron. There is a lot of recognition. There are maybe 20-25 others there.*

R: Okay!

S: *Almost all the others are in purple colours, but some are pink purple. We seldom meet.*

R: What kind of group is this?

S: *The first graders!*

R: The first graders?

S: *No, but in some way, we have been around for a very long time, but we have other purposes now. Somehow, we are a group and we have been companions for a very long time.*

R: Is it some kind of soul group?

S: *Yes, something like that.*

R: What do you have in common in this group?

S: *What?*

R: Do you have something in common?

S: *The word I get is truth! But I do not know.*

We continue, later in the conversation, to talk about the Surgeon.

S: *Avron understands. She holds my left hand.*

R: Why do you think she does that?

S: *Well ... love maybe. I don't know. It does not feel ... it is not wrong.*

R: How do you feel now?

S: *Yes! They say: "Do not be afraid of religion". "Religion is an opium." "Woman is soon free."*

R: Can you explain this about "women are soon free? I'd like to understand what you mean now with these short sentences.

S: *No worries! There is no woman who is below a man. And no man who is above a woman. They both sit side by side.*

R: Like you and Avron! Aha, thank you!

S: *Yes, so why should earth be any different? There is no need for religions. It will hurt, but there is no need for religion. "Freedom comes!" This is what they say! Well, I don't know —*

but these are things that do not affect me. These are larger flows of things. These are large events, so it is not my small group that takes care of that. It is something we already know. I know it and it will take time. But we will get there!

R: Thank you for sharing all this information! Would it be possible to ask about those who choose the road of violence and blow themselves up as suicide missions? Why would a soul choose "a violent road", do you think?

S: *The words I get are "confusion of the ego". And then "delusion of religion". There are those who blow themselves to pieces... well let's see... one can do this for many reasons. Sometimes one can do it ... well, earth is still a place of war sometimes ... very much ...*

Oh, now lots of information is pouring in ...

In some cases, you can blow yourself to pieces, because there is a purpose behind it. It is more about saving one's comrades in a battle, or that kind of situation. One chooses that road to save many of one's own. It sounds strange, but there can be a good cause behind it. However, what happens in the name of religion feels like ... a discomfort and they are very, very lost souls. But they still have ... the souls are not ... they are confused souls, but they have a purpose, still a higher cause ... oh, it is difficult to receive all this information ... in the long run ...

something new comes, that I can say. Good things will come out of it in the long run. There is a good cause in the long run. It must be revealed. It takes time.

This LBL session is about three hours with the surgeon in deep hypnosis. Before we finish, I ask him if there is a last minute message from Avron.

R: Is there a message from Avron before we take you back to the here and now as the Surgeon?

S: *She only gives me some kind of tap on the cheek again. Goodbye! And now she is gone.*

A letter from the Surgeon
after the second LBL

Hi Rita!

Concerning the suicide bombers that I was talking about in my second LBL and concerning a "better" cause: A situation I had in mind is for example "kamikaze pilots". Perhaps they are forced to do it, or they choose to do it, but most often it affects "the enemies".

Another scenario is a group of soldiers who are in a hopeless situation with an enemy, when one of the group members takes on a suicidal mission (with or without bombs) to try to save the group. For sure it is possible to imagine many examples concerning this. It most often happens to combatants and not civilians on a large scale.

Concerning sacrifice in the name of "religion": They are often confused souls who do this – striking at others without any discrimination, for example by a road, a marketplace, a mosque, a subway ... Many innocent civilians are affected.

The higher cause is to slowly awaken humankind to the fact that violence is not a feasible way to act and, over time, we will use these kinds of acts less and less. We are not there yet, unfortunately. The lost souls are taken care of.

I hope my explanation of what I said in my LBL will help you in your writing!

Warm regards
The Surgeon

After his first LBL and experience of being the soldier Ray, the Surgeon still had not let go of his longing for military life. A few months after his second LBL, he contacted me again for a third LBL. This time he said that all was well and he felt he was on the right track in his life again. His feeling of increased vulnerability was gone. He said that he had finally experienced a "farewell to arms" during a military training for Medical Doctors. In a moment when he was holding a machine gun, he thought: "Enough is enough, no more military life for me". He put down the machine gun and left the training.

A letter from the Surgeon
after his third LBL

My conviction is that this is my experience. Maybe I will be able to share it with others, but never fully convince them of its accuracy. It has connected me on a deep level with myself. A piece that I had missed has fallen into place.

For me there is a "before" and an "after" regarding this experience. There is nothing I can change, but it only gave me a true knowing and sincere peace during the experience. Anyhow, there is no need to blow my horn about it – because it is my experienced truth and nobody else's.

I can also see that throughout history there have been individuals who have surely conveyed similar experiences to others, strongly, as well as free from ego. Some of these people have probably in a good way, or perhaps sometimes in a bad way, become the foundation of movements and maybe even the birth of religions.

Based on my experience, I can understand people who have described similar experiences in this field, that lie beyond what we most often are able to experience with our five senses. It is all about the understanding of the unique journey of everyone, rather than the same way for everybody, but the power of this will grow by itself in everyone.

So again, this is something I carry inside, as a source for comfort and rest, and a truth that both enriches my life and helps me appreciate life as such. In other words: "All are called upon, all are chosen, but what makes us different from each other is the time and insight".

Finally, it is my absolute conviction that the time of formal religions is over, and that they are about to slowly disappear. How we will honor life and the unknown ahead will be revealed, but the dogma within religions belongs to history.

PART 6

Conclusion

Man is originally characterized by his "search for meaning" rather than his "search for himself." The more he forgets himself—giving himself to a cause or another person—the more human he is. And the more he is immersed and absorbed in something or someone other than himself the more he really becomes himself.

Viktor E. Frankl: *Man's Search for Ultimate Meaning*

My LBL journey started in October 2012 with a week of training in a beautiful mansion on the English countryside, where I shared magical moments with my teachers, co-teachers and fellow students from all over the world. During the week of training I felt like coming home both privately and professionally.

A few months after my training I certified and became a member of The Newton Institute. The high ethical and professional standards of this organization filled me with joy, responsibility and pride. Clients from all over Sweden, Norway, Finland and the Baltic states found me on the TNI website under "locate a therapist" and I could get to work.

In my first LBL I clearly felt myself in a past life reliving my last minutes and death as a little girl in the concentration camp of Bergen-Belsen. As horrible as the circumstances where, what meant the most to me was the love I felt from the young man who held me in his arms when I died. He was a living skeleton with his burning eyes looking at me. In war and in all challenging conditions what makes us greater than ourselves is the act of love. My first LBL gave my life a new truth and meaning. In my second LBL I came to terms with my tendency to burn out. My experience as Dr. Helen helped me to meet my own needs. I learned from the life as a dying and starving child in a concentration camp and from Dr. Helen who died so dry and malnourished that physical, emotional and spiritual nourishment is very important for me in this life. As an LBL facilitator I also use this wisdom about nourishment when I meet clients who have lost their igniting spark and who are longing for inner fulfillment. Many of my clients have all they can ask for, money, success, good health, happy marriage and lovely children. Still they tell me that there is something missing. In their LBL they often find their answers from within.

I also had a third LBL in June 2017 at the first TNI World Conference in Maryland, US. Again I was deeply healed on so many levels, and it was also wonderful to meet 40 LBL colleagues from all over the world during the conference week. We exchanged experiences and attended interesting workshops and of course had great fun together.

I have realized that working as an LBL facilitator is not the same as anything I have done before privately or in my career as a health professional and therapist. Each client comes with the urge to meet their soul. They bring many important existential questions to the occasion. A lot of preparation for the client and myself and a focused soulful awareness is the key to success. Every session consumes a lot of energy from me as well. To be of service I must take full responsibility for my own balance in life. This is the reason why I live and also work in the countryside close to Mother Nature where I can feel her heartbeat. Gardening and a daily practise of yoga and meditation is nourishing, as well as taking time off for myself. Since childhood I love to be around animals and my four cats teach me how to play, relax and live in the moment.

Since 2012 my life has become easier in the sense that my intuition has become stronger, which is like an inner compass. On the other hand it can be difficult to completely trust my intuition and to give up "the little me". To follow my inner guidance usually means that I do not always know consciously why I do certain things. This book project is an example of such inner guidance. I had never written a book before and had no idea how to do it either. Out of the blue one morning in January 2015 I started to write not knowing really why. As time went by, my book project seemed to carry an energy and drive of its own. For long periods nothing happened and I thought it was the end of it, but then I met someone or had a dream or vision which ignited the spark and the manuscript came alive again. Slowly the energy of my book and my own life journey came together in June, 2018.

Since I started to work with LBL, I have facilitated hundreds of sessions. All my clients bring a gift of love. In every single session I gather experience, knowledge and wisdom about the journey for that particular soul. Truly amazing every time. As a Newton Institute ambassador in Sweden, I feel the spirit of Dr. Michael Newton and my LBL colleagues standing by me in every session.

Life is a mystery, everyone must stand alone
I hear you call my name
And it feels like home

MADONNA: *LIKE A PRAYER*

Letters from LBL clients

In 2013, I read Journey of Souls by Michael Newton. I realized, to my great pleasure, there was an LBL facilitator in Sweden, so I booked time for a session as soon as I could.

It was incredibly overwhelming to get in touch with my soul in deep regression. The most memorable from this LBL was the meeting with my Guide, who had followed me in aeons. The feeling I had earlier, that he was around me, became so real after the session and continues to affect me and supports me in daily life.

After a few years, it was time for a new LBL session. I had no special questions I wanted to answer, but I trusted that I would come into contact with things of importance for my continued development. In this long session, I got an explanation of the horror and concern I experienced as an 11-year-old. One of my teachers had told me that another planet could crash with the earth in the coming year and humanity would go under. This experience had led to strong emotions, which were stored in my subconscious mind and created an inner stress during my life. Rita led me so well into a life in connection with the fall of Atlantis. In that life, there were explanations I needed, to get an overall picture of the experiences I had.

Rita and I started writing books at the same time. But it became a stop in my flow and creativity after a while. During the session, I got a clear guide on how to proceed.

I am very grateful for that and for such warm and loving guidance of Rita to get in touch with my soul.

Ann-Christine Magnusson
Sweden

Rita asks me questions and I tell her everything I experience, even though it is quite difficult to speak when I am deeply hypnotized. It feels like someone is disturbing me just before I am about to fall asleep. But I just tell her the first thought I have and do not bother to analyze it.

When deeply relaxed on Rita's couch with Nelly, the cat sleeping beside me, I have an inner vision that I am building a house or a temple with my father. It is a huge stone building and I am standing three meters above the ground. I handle large blocks of stone raised by huge ropes from father, who stands on the ground. I feel very strong, happy and full of hope.

Rita then asks me to go to another positive event in the same life. I see myself as a teacher in astronomy and I see young students sitting on the sandy ground busy making calculations. Everything is about mathematics and the positions of the stars. My students make calculations using sticks for drawing in the sand and I walk around pointing at things they have done.

We are now in the same temple that I built with my father when I was 18 years old. He taught me everything I know and I am walking in his footsteps as a teacher. By the entrance to the temple there is a huge compass on the ground. It is made of white stone. It reminds me of the importance of sunrise and sunset.

Now Rita asks me to go to the last day of my life as an astronomer, and I feel safe to do this when I hear her soft voice with a slight Finnish accent. I hover above myself and I see the whole scene from the upper corner of the ceiling. I am not sad and it rather feels like realizing that I am dead now. The room is filled with huge white flowers like in a ceremony. The next moment I fly straight upwards in an enormous speed, then slowing down, but I soon continue in high speed again. When I finally stop moving my father, who died before me is there to welcome me with open arms. I feel happy and comfortable.

Ehva Löpp
www.ehvalopp.se
Sweden

For more than 30 years I have helped people develop, to find balance and functionality. I realized that the uncomplicated but often natural inside of us, can be hard to find. My LBL session with

Rita is undoubtedly the greatest experience for me to find this simplicity in myself. Moreover, it is important for me to have my own personal experience, in my way.

Rita "held my hand" in a calm and warm way. I felt absolutely safe. The session was a new start for me both as a human being and as a professional.

Hans Mazolaqi
Master and founder of Energiologi
www.energiologi.se
Sweden and Spain

The LBL journey was such a delight for me and especially my soul. My body and mind could just rest calmly on Rita's couch listening to the warm fire, restful but still fully awake, and it was so wonderful to let my soul, communicate directly, without going through the mind in this way. The communication was so authentic, direct, sometimes very surprising, interesting and soothing, not having to think ahead, analyse or ponder about anything. I was so present, witnessing the communication between Rita and my soul, on this journey not knowing what would come next and just responding as Rita guided me through this journey with her questions.

Anne L.

What a WASTE!

Past Life Experience

Letter from my LBL colleague Stephen Sauvage in Australia

When I read about the past life of the Surgeon it reminded me about my past life on the Somme ...

It began being in the trenches on the Somme as a British Soldier. I am looking up at the morning sky, lit up with flashes of cannon fire. Next, we are lined up on the edges of the trenches about to go over the top to charge the enemy.

Then I'm floating above my body looking down at a pair of hands, pushing my intestines back inside of me. Then there is an unbearable sense of sadness. I have tears flowing down my cheers as I look across the field of battle at the bodies of my dead comrades.

What a waste of life of these young men.

How senseless this war is! As I move from this life I notice in the distance amongst all the death and mud is a white building standing all alone, a farmhouse I think?

I had an amazing insight into myself as to why I have doubted my courage at times, have a distaste for violence and have walked away from violent altercations and yet have played very physical sport. I have never been afraid to protect others or myself when required such as entering a burning house to get people out or assisting in emergencies.

~

The Newton Institute
Code of Ethics

~

All of the certified Life Between Lives hypnotherapists listed on **www.newtoninstitute.org** operate to the very highest standards of ethics and behavior which are set out below:

In the sacred quest to provide a meaningful Life Between Lives (LBL) experience, practitioners use all of their skills, training, and experience to reconnect their clients to the loving wisdom of the spirit world. In recognition of the intuitive nature of LBL facilitation, practitioners remain open to spiritual guidance when conducting sessions.

Practitioners provide their clients with a safe and

caring professional environment. The profound trust inherent in the client-practitioner relationship is respected, and therefore each LBL session is conducted with courtesy, sensitivity, and patience.

Informed consent is always obtained from clients after imparting clearly and honestly the range of experiences that may be realized in an LBL session. Financial policies are declared in advance, and fee arrangements are resolved before beginning a session.

Individual advertising and promotional campaigns are truthful, and realistic statements are made regarding client outcomes. Personal qualifications are communicated clearly; factual information on relevant certifications and professional affiliations is fully disclosed to clients and prospective clients upon request.

Complete confidentiality is honored and maintained for each client, as well as for the spiritual beings who may come forth in an LBL session. All client-practitioner communications are confidential. Client permission must be granted when recording a session and when sharing or publishing session material. Records are preserved in a secure environment to ensure privacy.

The purity of LBL therapy as a stand-alone discipline is protected. When offering non-LBL services during the course of LBL therapy, practitioners advise clients that such services are beyond the explicit endorsement of The Newton Institute.

In order to expand the understanding and practice of LBL therapy, practitioners may share session records with The Newton Institute's research department after appropriate permissions have been obtained. Practitioners stay informed of new advances in the field by participating in LBL eGroups, attending Institute trainings, conducting research, and pursuing other relevant educational opportunities whenever possible.

Practitioners honor collegial relationships by cooperating with all of The Newton Institute's officials and members. Practitioners speak respectfully of colleagues, and will not solicit another practitioner's clients.

As ambassadors of The Newton Institute, practitioners work to illuminate public awareness regarding LBL therapy. Practitioners conduct themselves in such a manner as to uphold the integrity of LBL therapy and The Newton Institute above any individual.

Find a therapist trained by The Newton Institute

If you are interested in having an LBL session, please go to the Newton Institute official website on www.newtoninstitute.org and click on "locate a therapist".

In May 2018, we have 204 LBL facilitators listed in 44 countries and 24 languages. We are all trained by The Newton Institute (TNI) to carry on the legacy of Dr. Michael Newton.

TNI offers new case studies by members and updated information about LBL in our newsletter called "Stories of the Afterlife" which you can subscribe on the TNI website.

TNI is a non-profit organization with highly developed standards based on the Code of Ethics.

Acknowledgements

Thank you Surgeon whose case story is told in this book. You have also provided me with letters, proofreading and honest feedback.

Thank you dear Engineer for your great contribution to this book. Although I did not use your case study as I planned and told you, your input was important and I hope you will enjoy the outcome.

Thank you Karen Joy, Alan and Mary Channer, Birgitta Lind and Leo Padazakos for your help with proofreading and feedback.

Specially thank you Ann-Christine Magnusson for supporting me with your wisdom and astrological professional and personal advice through my ups and downs during the process of writing. Thank you for your proofreading until the very last minute. I felt your company all along the way like a powerful guardian angel. Thank you for your letter about your session.

Thank you Dr. Dorothea Fuckert for sharing your experience as M.D., LBL colleague and author. Thank you for your loving foreword.

Thank you Pete Smith for your support as LBL colleague and author. It is always so uplifting to be in touch with you. Thank you for your kind foreword.

Thank you Ehva Löpp and Hans Mazolaqi for sharing your interesting LBL experience.

Thank you LBL colleague Stephen Sauvage for sharing your past life story.

Thank you Terry Evans for your support and loving kindness. Thank you for the personal message you share on the back of my book.

Thank you Ann-Sofie Hammarström Östergren for your creative visual magic to make my manuscript into a real book.

Thank you Marianne Philp, for introducing me to Ann-Sofie Hammarström Östergren when you heard about my book project.

Thank you Yngve Jansson for always supporting me with love and wisdom.

Thank you my kind brother Ariel Borenstein for standing by me since the day I was born.

Further reading

Books by Dr. Michael Newton:
    Journey of Souls, 1994
    Destiny of Souls, 2002
    Life between Lives Hypnotherapy for spiritual regression, 2011

Books by The Newton Institute:
    Memories of Afterlife, 2011

The Newton Institute Website:
    www.newtoninstitute.org

The Rita Borenstein Website:
    www.spiritualregression.se

Books about LBL by TNI members:
Karen Joy: *Other Lives Other Realms*, 2015
Dorothea Fuckert: *Seelenreise in das Leben zwischen den Leben*, 2013

More recommended reading

Pete Smith: *Quantum Consciousness – Expanding your personal universe,* 2015.

Yonassan Gershom: *Beyond the Ashes – Cases of Reincarnation from the Holocaust November,* 1992

Jane Roberts: *All her 24 books,* 1958 – 1997, dictated by Seth (spirit) and notes by Robert F. Butts

Books by Dr. Eben Alexander: *Proof of Heaven – A neurosurgeon's search into afterlife,* 2012
Map of Heaven – How science, religion and ordinary people are proving the afterlife, 2014

Dr. Eben Alexander and Karen Newell: *Living in a mindful Universe – A neurosurgeon's journey into the heart of consciousness,* 2017